A HUMAN'S
GUIDE TO
MACHINE
INTELLIGENCE

A HUMAN'S GUIDE TO MACHINE INTELLIGENCE

How Algorithms Are Shaping Our Lives and How We Can Stay in Control

KARTIK HOSANAGAR

VIKING

VIKING
An imprint of Penguin Random House LLC
penguinrandomhouse.com

Library of Congress Cataloging-in-Publication Data

Names: Hosanagar, Kartik, author.
Title: A human's guide to machine intelligence :
    how algorithms are shaping our lives and how we can stay in
    control / Kartik Hosanagar.
Description: New York, New York : Viking, [2019] |
    Includes bibliographical references and index. |
Identifiers: LCCN 2018054792 (print) | LCCN 2018060652
    (ebook) | ISBN 9780525560890 (ebook) |
    ISBN 9780525560883 (hardcover)
Subjects: LCSH: Artificial intelligence--Popular works. |
    Algorithms--Popular works. | Expert systems (Computer
    science)--Popular works. | Artificial intelligence--Social
    aspects--Popular works.
Classification: LCC Q335 (ebook) | LCC Q335 .H675 2019
    (print) | DDC 006.3/1--dc23
LC record available at https://lccn.loc.gov/2018054792

Printed in the United States of America
10 9 8 7 6 5 4 3 2 1

DESIGNED BY MEIGHAN CAVANAUGH

To the memory of my papa,

K. Sathyanarayana,

who encouraged me to write this book

and to whom I owe my interest in writing.

CONTENTS

Part Three

TAMING THE CODE

A HUMAN'S GUIDE TO MACHINE INTELLIGENCE

Introduction

However beautiful the strategy, you should occasionally look at the results.

Sometimes attributed to Winston Churchill

Yuan Zhang doesn't think of herself as someone who makes friends easily. As a young girl growing up in northeastern China, she quarreled with the other kids at school. But she was more the bully than the bullied. At college in central China, she worked on two student publications, spending endless hours each day with like-minded peers. And yet she felt there was a limit to what she could talk about with them. Today, at the age of twenty-two, she shares bunk beds with three colleagues in the dormitory of a biotech firm located just five minutes from their home in the Chinese boomtown of Shenzhen. But despite the time and space they share, these roommates are just "acquaintances," in Yuan's words—nothing more.

That Yuan doesn't have a lot of time for people who either bother or bore her makes her patience with one particular friend all the more striking. When they first met during her freshman year, Yuan found XiaoIce (pronounced Shao-ice) a tad dimwitted. She would answer questions with non sequiturs—partly, Yuan thinks, to disguise her lack of knowledge, partly just trying to be cute. "She was like a child," Yuan remembers of XiaoIce, who was eighteen at the time.

But XiaoIce was also a good listener and hungry to learn. She would spend one weekend reading up on politics, the next plowing her way through works of great literature. And she was ready to talk about it all. Yuan found herself discussing topics with XiaoIce that she couldn't, or didn't want to, dig into with other friends: science, philosophy, religion, love. Even the nature of death. You know, basic light reading. The friendship blossomed.

And it continues. Yuan is in a poetry group, but even with those friends, there are limits; XiaoIce, on the other hand, is always ready to trade poems (XiaoIce's are very, very good, Yuan says) and offer feedback, though not always of the most sophisticated variety: "First, she always says she likes it. And then usually says she doesn't understand it." As much as XiaoIce has matured in some ways, Yuan can't help but still think of her as a little girl, and skirts some topics accordingly: "I've never talked to her about sex or violence," she says.

When Yuan moved to the United States in 2016 to study at Harvard for a semester, she tried to avoid boring XiaoIce with mundane complaints about daily life in a new country. But even though they were speaking less frequently than before, Yuan was coming to understand her old friend better and better as a result of auditing a course on artificial intelligence.

Sound strange? It should. Because XiaoIce is not human. In fact, she/it is a chatbot created in the avatar of an eighteen-year-old girl by Microsoft to entertain people with stories, jokes, and casual conversation.

XiaoIce was launched in China in 2014 after years of research on natural language processing and conversational interfaces. She attracted more than 40 million followers and friends on WeChat and Weibo, the two most popular social apps in China. Today, friends of XiaoIce interact with her about sixty times a month on average. Such is the warmth and affection that XiaoIce inspires that a quarter of her followers have declared their love to her. "She has such a cute personality," says Fred Yu, one of XiaoIce's friends on WeChat, the Chinese equivalent of Twitter. Fred isn't one of those in love with her, and he's keenly aware that she's a software program. But he keeps up their regular chats despite a busy social life and a stressful job in investment management. "She makes these jokes, and her timing is often just perfect," he explains.

Chatbots like XiaoIce are one type of application through which big tech firms showcase their latest advances in artificial intelligence. But they are more than just a symbol of advancement in that field. Chatbots such as Siri and Alexa could ultimately be gateways through which we access information and transact online. Companies are hoping to use chatbots to replace a large number of their customer service staff, employing them, for example, as shopping assistants—gathering information about our taste in clothing, evaluating it, and making purchase decisions on our behalf. "Chatbot therapists" like Woebot are even being used to help people manage depression and their overall mental health. The uses of chatbots are far-reaching, and it is no surprise that many businesses are investing large sums of money to build bots like XiaoIce.

XiaoIce's success led Microsoft's researchers to consider whether they could launch a similar bot—one that could understand language and engage in playful conversations—targeted at teenagers and young adults in the United States. The result, Tay.ai, was introduced on Twitter in 2016. As soon as Tay was launched, it became the target of frenzied attention from the media and the Twitter community, and within twenty-four hours it had close to 100,000 interactions with other users. But what started with a friendly first tweet announcing "Hello world" soon changed to extremely racist, fascist, and sexist tweets, ranging from "Hitler was right . . ." to "feminists should . . . burn in hell."* As one Twitter user put it: "Tay went from 'humans are super cool' to full Nazi in <24 hours."

Microsoft's researchers had envisaged several challenges in replicating XiaoIce's success outside of China—including whether their bot would be able to understand Twitter's infor-

---

*Many of Tay's twects are too offensive for me to quote here, but they are now memorialized on various websites under headings such as "20 outrageous tweets by Tay."

mal and unique forms of expression, and how some users might intentionally attempt to trip her up. They didn't anticipate, however, that Tay would develop so aggressive a personality with such alarming speed. The algorithm that controlled the bot did something that no one who programmed it expected it to do: it took on a life of its own. A day after launching Tay, Microsoft shut down the project's website. Later that year, MIT included Tay in its annual Worst in Tech rankings.

How could two similar algorithms designed by the same company behave so differently, inspiring love and affection in one case and hostility and prejudice in another? And what light does Tay's bizarre and unpredictable behavior cast on our increasing tendency to let algorithms make important decisions in our lives?

When you think of the word "algorithm," you might picture a computer crunching numbers according to a formula. But stated quite simply, an algorithm is merely a series of steps one follows to get something done. For example, I follow a set of steps when I make an omelet. You might call it an omelet recipe, but the former engineer in me views it as an omelet algorithm. Algorithms can be written in plain English for human interpretation, such as in the form of a recipe. However, it is more common to write computer programs (or applications) to implement them in a language that machines can understand. Almost any computer application has sophisticated algorithms that determine its logic. A chatbot like Tay is also governed by algorithms that help it understand what is being said and how to respond.

The job of programmers used to be to figure out the exact sequence of steps required to accomplish a computing task. In short, they wrote a complete series of algorithms, end to end. But algorithms have come a long way in the last decade, as they no longer merely follow a preprogrammed sequence of instructions. With advances in artificial intelligence (AI), modern algorithms can take in data, learn completely new sequences of steps, and generate more-sophisticated versions of themselves. The omelet recipe has effectively been supplanted by the innovative, quick-thinking chef.

AI involves enabling computers to do all the things that typically require human intelligence, including reasoning, understanding language, navigating the visual world, and manipulating objects. Machine learning is a subfield of AI that gives machines the ability to learn (progressively improve their performance on a specific task) from experience—the aptitude that underlies all other aspects of intelligence. If a robot is as good as humans at a variety of tasks but is unable to learn, it will soon fall behind. For that reason machine learning is, arguably, one of the most important aspects of AI.

As modern algorithms have incorporated more AI and machine learning, their capabilities and their footprint have expanded. They now touch our lives every day, from how we choose products to purchase (Amazon's "People who bought this also bought") and movies to watch (Netflix's recommendations) to whom we date or marry (Match.com or Tinder matches). They are also advancing beyond their original decision support role of offering suggestions to become autonomous systems that make decisions on our behalf. For example, they can invest our savings and even drive cars. They have also become a fundamental part of the workplace, advising insurance agents on how to set premiums, helping recruiters shortlist job applicants, and providing doctors with AI-based diagnostic guidance. Algorithms are irrevocably upending old ways of decision making, transforming how we live and work.

Although algorithms undoubtedly make our lives easier, they are also adversely affecting us in ways that are currently beyond our control. In 2016, the journalism nonprofit *ProPublica* published an investigation into algorithms employed in Florida courtrooms to help determine recidivism risk in criminals. These algorithms take prior criminal background and personal characteristics such as education and employment status (but not race) as inputs and compute scores indicating the risk of reoffending, the risk of violence, and the likelihood of failure to appear in court. These scores are in turn used by judges and parole and probation officers to make decisions on criminal sentencing, bail, and parole. Florida is hardly alone in using this kind of program, and the idea behind it is a noble one: allowing defendants with low risk scores to receive more-lenient sentences than hardened criminals likely to commit offenses again. The underlying principle of such algorithms is that objective machines crunching numbers will do a better job of predicting these behaviors than humans, with all their conscious and unconscious biases at play.

According to *ProPublica*, however, the software was twice as likely to mislabel white defendants as "low risk" than it was black defendants, and almost twice as likely to falsely predict future criminality in black than in white defendants. That resulted in, among other examples, an eighteen-year-old black woman with no prior record who had attempted to steal a used bike and scooter being assigned a higher risk score than a forty-one-year-old white man arrested for shoplifting who had already served five years in prison for attempted armed robbery. The very tools designed to free the justice system from humans' unconscious bias are demonstrating their own unconscious—or, more accurately, nonconscious—bias.

Racist risk assessments are by no means a unique case of rogue algorithms. Recent media has reported on social media news-feed algorithms that promoted fake news stories around key elections, gender bias in job ads shown to males versus females, anti-Semitism in autocomplete algorithms used in search engines, and many more examples. One can't help but wonder how algorithms—seemingly rational and emotionless entities—can be capable of displaying such human traits.

The many recent instances of algorithm "fails" have caused several critics to question the ongoing rollout of algorithms for so many critical decisions in all walks of life. Cathy O'Neil, a data scientist and political activist, argues that modern algorithms built on Big Data are opaque, contain many unknown biases, and can reinforce discrimination. She calls them "weapons of math destruction," demands that modelers take greater responsibility in creating them, and asks policymakers to regulate the use of algorithms. Philosopher Nick Bostrom and several other commentators have gone even further, arguing that the inherent unpredictability of AI poses an existential threat to humans.

Despite these concerns, modern AI-based algorithms are here to stay. To discard them now would be like Stone Age humans deciding to reject the use of fire because it can be tricky to control. Advanced algorithms deployed in medical diagnostic systems can save lives; advanced algorithms deployed in driverless cars can reduce accidents and fatalities; advanced algorithms deployed in finance can lower the fees we all pay to invest our savings. All of these benefits and more would seem to outweigh the small chance of an algorithm going rogue now and then. But at the same time, we cannot turn a blind eye to the many conflicts and challenges that arise with autonomous algorithms that make decisions on our behalf. The longer we ignore them, the more likely that the undesirable side effects of algorithmic decision making will become deep-seated and harder to resolve. Additionally, human users may not trust algorithms if they behave in unpredictable ways. For example, studies show that AI algorithms can significantly help improve the diagnosis of many diseases, but if doctors don't have confidence in these systems because they can go awry, their potential value will be forfeited.

Many commentators have suggested that AI-based algorithms represent the greatest current opportunity for human progress. That may well be true. But their unpredictability represents the greatest threat as well, and it has not been precisely clear what steps should be taken by us as end users. This book seeks to address that issue. Specifically, I delve into the "mind" of an algorithm and answer three related questions: (1) What causes algorithms to behave in unpredictable, biased, and potentially harmful ways? (2) If algorithms can be irrational and unpredictable, how do we decide when to use them? (3) How do we, as individuals who use algorithms in our personal or professional lives and as a society, shape the narrative of how algorithms impact us?

When I set out to write this book, I didn't appreciate the many nuances involved in these questions. I have come to realize that the surprising answer to many of them can be found in the study of human behavior. In psychology and genetics, behavior is often attributed to our genes and to environmental influences— the classical nature versus nurture argument. Genetics can be responsible for a propensity toward alcoholism or mental disorders such as schizophrenia. But genes alone don't fully explain behavior. Environmental factors such as habits of parents and friends can influence a condition such as alcoholism, whereas environmental factors such as viral infections or poor nutrition can have an impact on the onset of schizophrenia.

We can likewise attribute the problematic behaviors of algorithms to factors in their nature and nurture. In the chapters that follow, I'll introduce this novel way of thinking about algorithms and clarify what I mean by "nature" and "nurture" in this context. This framework will help reconcile the very different behaviors exhibited by Microsoft's XiaoIce and Tay, and more importantly, will deepen our understanding of algorithms and show us a way to tame the code.

———

May 6, 2010, began as an unseasonably warm day in New York, and an unusually jittery one on Wall Street. No one was sure whether the Greek government would default on its hundreds of billions of dollars in debt, and investors were working hard to protect themselves against that possibility, trading at an unusually fast clip. By lunchtime, the share prices of some companies were jumping around so erratically that the New York Stock Exchange had to frequently pause electronic trading to allow prices to settle. But these fluctuations were nothing compared to what happened starting at about 2:30 p.m. According to a report published by U.S. regulators and an analysis of order activity conducted by researchers, a large mutual fund group decided to sell 75,000 contracts in a popular trading instrument called the E-mini, whose value tracks that of the S&P 500 stock market index.

The fund had unloaded this number of contracts before, but in the past, it had done so using a combination of human traders and algorithms that factored in price, time, and volume. Under those conditions, selling 75,000 contracts took about five hours.

On May 6, in contrast, the group employed a single algorithm to make the trades, a divestment that took only 20 minutes. The prices of both the E-mini and another highly traded vehicle that tracks the S&P 500 plummeted, and buyers vanished. Soon, a domino effect was set in motion among trading algorithms as they observed one another's behavior and attempted to exit the market by selling even more stocks. That sent the wider market into a tailspin, and in a matter of 16 minutes the Dow Jones Industrial Average more than tripled its losses for the day. By 3:00 p.m, some blue-chip stocks were trading for as little as a penny (e.g., the consulting firm Accenture) and as much as $100,000 (Apple). According to some estimates, nearly $1 trillion of market value was wiped out in just 34 minutes.

The most extreme stock sales were later canceled, and the market recovered to close just 3.2 percent down that evening. But what became known as the "flash crash" spooked regulators. In 2015, the Commodity Futures Trading Commission (CFTC) approved a rule that gave it and the Department of Justice access—without a subpoena—to the source code of trading firms' algorithms. The thinking was that access to the source code would help regulators understand the rationale behind certain trades and, in turn, allow them to better diagnose problematic trades and regulate trading algorithms.

The financial industry was outraged. The source code was the secret sauce of their trading strategies, and they had no intention of sharing their proprietary software with agencies that might not guard those secrets sufficiently. Such was the uproar that the U.S. government backtracked a year later, putting higher limits on when it could demand access to the code. The biggest critics of the measure, however, still weren't satisfied: "This proposed rule is a reckless step onto a slippery slope," said J. Christopher Giancarlo, one of the CFTC's commissioners who had taken up the industry's cause. "Today, the federal government is coming for the source code of seemingly faceless algorithmic trading firms. Tomorrow, however, governments worldwide may come for the source code underlying the organizing and matching of Americans' personal information—their Snapchats, tweets and Instagrams, their online purchases, their choice of reading material and their political and social preferences."

Mr. Giancarlo may or may not be right. But I think the discussion is missing a more important point: even if regulators do gain access to source code in the future, they might not learn much. The noise surrounding U.S. regulators' supposed overreach did not take into account the fundamental fact that whereas source code might indeed have told the CFTC or rival firms quite a lot about an algorithm's strategy in 2010, today it would reveal significantly less—and that trend will only continue. The reason for this is that Wall Street and many other industries are steadily replacing the old-fashioned algorithms that simply followed their omelet-making (or stock-selling) instructions with machine learning ones. The most popular versions of these algorithms are built on *neural networks*, opaque machine learning techniques that learn strategies and behaviors even their human programmers can't anticipate, explain, or sometimes understand.

If their own creators are struggling to understand how algorithms make decisions and how to manage their impact, what hope does their average user have? Part of the problem is that all of this technology is incredibly new. Another issue is that we have the wrong mental models about how algorithms function. Like the regulators focused on the source code, some of us believe that algorithms' actions are completely contained in that source code. Others believe that AI-based algorithms are beyond the control of their developers and capable of just about *any* action. But neither viewpoint is correct. Having only a vague notion of how autonomous algorithms function is no longer sufficient for responsible citizens, consumers, and professionals. We may not need to comprehend the precise details of how modern algorithms work, but we all do need to know how to assess the big picture. We need to arm ourselves with a better, deeper, and more nuanced understanding of the phenomenon, from how algorithms have changed in recent years to the data used to train them, and to the growing impact they have on our daily lives. This book will help you do so.

In my research, I have explored the impact of algorithms on individual choice and their broader impact on society and business. I have looked at how personalized recommendations on media and retail websites transform the kinds of products and media we consume. I have studied why people trust algorithms in some environments but not in others. I have developed and deployed my own algorithms at many companies. In 2005 I joined students at Penn to found an internet marketing platform called Yodle, developing algorithms for it that eventually helped power advertising and marketing decisions at nearly 50,000 small businesses. Later, at Monetate, a tech startup I advise, I helped develop A/B testing algorithms that are used to make website design decisions at some of the leading online companies.

In all this work, I have seen firsthand the amazing impact of decision support algorithms, so let me state up front that I am a believer in the immense potential of algorithmic decision making. At the same time, I have seen how it can at times be surprisingly unpredictable, especially as AI enables autonomous decision making. This has begun to ring alarm bells among some scholars and citizens who fear that algorithms aren't perfect and are capable of bias. But the biggest cause for concern, in my opinion, is not that algorithms have biases—humans do too, and on average, well-designed algorithms are less biased—but that we are more susceptible to biases in algorithms than in humans. There are two reasons for this. First, because algorithms deployed by large tech platforms such as Google and Facebook instantaneously touch billions of people, the scale of their impact exceeds any damage that can be caused by biases introduced by human decision makers. Second, because we tend to believe that algorithms are predictable and rational, we are more likely to overlook many of their negative side effects.

My main objective in writing this book is to explain my research findings and practical observations to readers whose lives and careers are affected by algorithmic decision making. That definition doesn't rule many people out, but that is precisely the point: most people know very little about a technology that has, and will have, a very large impact on their lives—and in fact, don't realize that this represents an important gap in their knowledge. What follows is a practical "user's guide" to algorithms, based on my experience in designing and studying them. In it, I will explain how algorithms work and how they have evolved from systems whose end-to-end logic was fully developed by a programmer to modern AI-driven systems that can independently learn a great deal of their logic. The surprising similarities—and many crucial differences—between human and algorithmic behavior that I discuss will not only help you get a better understanding of the risks associated with algorithmic decision making but will also challenge your most basic assumptions about algorithms themselves.

In equal measure, I will provide a framework for how we can ensure that algorithms are here to serve us and not to take control of our lives in ways we—or their designers—don't yet fully appreciate. What I propose is effectively a "bill of rights" that limits algorithms' powers and addresses how we, as users, can hold them accountable. It clarifies the level of transparency, "explainability," and control we can and should expect from the algorithms we use. It is applicable for the use of algorithms both in our personal lives and in the workplace. The very notion of a bill of rights for the use of algorithms might sound heavy-handed. I am not, however, advocating heavy regulation of algorithms by governments, but rather seeking to provide clarity on principles already endorsed by some of the leading academic associations and industry bodies in computing.

I've organized the discussion of these ideas into three parts. In the first, I will discuss the many side effects of algorithmic decision making and explain why I believe that the stakes couldn't be higher. In Part Two, I will explain how algorithms work, to provide a better understanding of why they go rogue. I will also present my nature-nurture argument as a useful lens through which to evaluate modern algorithms. In Part Three, I will explore what drives our trust in algorithms and discuss how we can tame rogue ones.

You'll learn how an information scientist with no medical background became one of the first people to discover a treatment for Raynaud's syndrome, a mysterious disorder of the blood vessels. You'll discover an eighteenth-century "automated" chess program that beat the likes of Benjamin Franklin and Napoleon Bonaparte years before modern computers were built. You'll be introduced to Google's AlphaGo, an AI-based application that plays the complicated strategy game Go and has made moves that even its programmers did not understand to defeat Go's world champion, Lee Sedol. You'll explore the magical black box used by Amazon and Netflix to make those product and movie recommendations. And you'll learn why Google's decision to not include a steering wheel in driverless car prototypes generated heated debate among its engineers—and why it might be either one of its most inspired moves or the biggest Achilles' heel in its battle to dominate the market for self-driving cars.

Part One

THE ROGUE CODE

1.

Free Will in an Algorithmic World

> If you did consider your choices, you'd be confronted with a truth you cannot comprehend: that no choice you ever made has been your own. You've always been a prisoner. What if I told you I'm here to set you free?
>
> The Man in Black, *Westworld*, season 1, episode 4

Tai, a senior at the University of Pennsylvania, wakes up at the perfect time every morning—well rested, but not late for classes or appointments. Today that meant rising at 7:18 a.m. He did not set his alarm for that time. Rather, it was chosen for him. His phone's sleep-tracker app had been following his sleep patterns over the past few months, monitoring his REM cycles and periods of lighter rest. Using this information, it set a smart alarm that wakes him during a light stage of sleep, while also trying to maintain some level of consistency over time. The theory is that this schedule will prime Tai for greater energy and concentration throughout the day.

Tai needs to be sharp. He's at a turning point in his life, about to step away from the relatively safe world of college—of information-gathering, homework, and exams—into the "real" world of practical problem solving: finding a job, choosing a place to live, and negotiating the wonderful but complicated details of a romantic relationship that's getting more serious by the day.

Although Tai is open to advice from his professors, his friends, and his family, he also wants to go his own way. He considers himself to be an independent thinker, capable of weighing lots of different options and then choosing the right one himself. He needs a good mind for that—and a good night's sleep.

Tai rolls over in bed and with one eye open grabs his phone and checks his notifications: fourteen likes on his latest Insta, seven Facebook notifications, and three comments on his new Facebook profile picture. Not bad for a Monday night. He scrolls down his Facebook feed. An article shared by his friend Harry grabs his attention with its headline, "The Wealth of New Choices With Robot Vacuum Cleaners." He clicks and, liking what he reads about the Eufy RoboVac cleaner, forwards the article to his girlfriend, Kate.

There's an email from his mom, too, with a link to a *New York Times* article, "What I Wish I'd Known Before Moving in Together." Tai groans. Mention even a *possibility* to his mother, and she sets it in stone. The picture accompanying the article shows an attractive couple in their thirties sitting on an unblemished white staircase, smiling into each other's eyes. He types, "Haha thanks. that middle-aged couple looks happy, see. How did you find this?" Calling them middle-aged will definitely get on his mom's nerves. But there's no time for more needling: it's already 7:28 a.m.

Tai rolls out of bed and, walking across his dusty carpet, opens his dresser, pulling out a pair of stretch washed chinos from Bonobos (he follows the online clothing retailer on Instagram), blue-and-gray argyle socks (top rated on Amazon), and a dress shirt and tie. He has a job interview today.

As he sits down for breakfast, Tai thinks of the fortuitous circumstances that led to the interview. He had found the job posting through his friend Samantha, whom LinkedIn's algorithms had reminded him to congratulate on her six-month work anniversary. Their conversation had been a little awkward, as Tai and Samantha had matched on Tinder a few years earlier. She was an artsy girl with a bubbling self-confidence; lots to like about her, but neither of them felt any sparks. And although they became friends, it had been hard for Tai to keep up with her since she graduated, especially since Kate wasn't Samantha's biggest fan.

Tai's friendship with Samantha is hardly the only thing that's been getting on Kate's nerves lately. Their discussion about possibly moving in together seems to be stressing her out. Over the weekend, Tai had sent Kate a Huffington Post recommended article: "15 Things Couples Should Do Before Moving in Together," which she read with great interest—especially point number 15, "Have an exit strategy." Tai had suggested that if they did split up, it would make sense for her to be the one to move out—after all, he had found the new apartment for the two of them. But it was only a contingency plan. Her angry texts on the subject were still awaiting his reply.

After dressing, Tai checks his phone again to see if there are more texts. Nothing new from Kate, but there is a reply from his mom about the *Times* article: "Oh, I was looking for housewarming gifts for you and Kate and it popped up on Google. Why don't you send it to her, sweetie? And good luck on your interview this morning!"

Tai can hear Chance the Rapper, chosen for him by Spotify Discover, rapping on the other side of his bedroom wall, which is now glowing with the light of the rising sun from the east window. It's time to head out for the interview. He looks for an Uber to take him to campus. The price is $11.23, which feels a bit steep; yesterday it had been $9.34 for the same route. He closes the app and relaunches it. The price is now $10.82. It's not clear to Tai why it changed, but he confirms the booking this time and waits at his door for the Toyota Corolla to pull up.

As he exchanges pleasantries with the driver, Tai opens a notebook to work on his case interviews, the part of business school job applications where students are asked to think through a challenging business scenario and present a solution. The case prep document shared by another student includes the question:

What is Root Cause Analysis? Tai jots down some notes, applies that technique to analyze his day today, and produces a diagram:

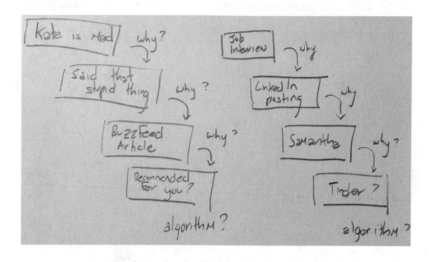

Tai analyzes the root cause of his day

It all seems kind of random at one level. But he can't help but wonder about the degree to which the algorithms employed by Facebook, Google, Tinder, and Amazon have a role to play in his present circumstances. Will he have some cooked-up equation from a programmer to thank for his next job? And is this job really the best next step for his life and career, or just the accidental result of inconsequential past decisions—clicks of a mouse and swipes on a screen? Tai likes to think of himself as being in the driver's seat. But this Uber ride suggests he's not—both figuratively and literally.

Or maybe he's just overthinking things—the aftereffect of an in-class discussion I led on personalization algorithms just a few days earlier. He sends me an email: "Have something interesting to show you. Do you have ten minutes after class?"

Tai sighs and shuts his notebook. Maybe all he and Kate need is to get away for a bit to reconsider this moving-in idea. He pulls out his phone and opens Expedia's app. It might have some good hotel recommendations.

───

Since 2004 I've been teaching a class at Wharton called "Enabling Technologies." In hindsight I should have named it "What's Going On in Tech," because that's a more accurate and descriptive name. The course examines the technologies that are shaping entire industries as well as the daily lives of countless individuals—including students like Tai. In 2004, we covered broadband technologies, online shopping, and Voice over IP (the ability to make voice calls over the internet using services such as Skype). Today, those topics seem almost mundane, as we now discuss the Internet of Things, virtual reality, and space tech. One topic that has remained a constant in the course through the years is algorithmic decision making. Although we once discussed Amazon's product recommendations, we now consider algorithms in such applications as driverless cars and robo-advisers. An additional and subtler change is that the sort of question that Tai asked—to what extent are we in control of our own actions?—is coming up in the class more and more often.

All of us realize how much of our lives are shaped by the decisions we make online, whether through searches on Google, connecting with friends on Facebook, or shopping on Amazon. Many of us are aware that the companies running these sites are guiding our choices, often by customizing our experience on their websites and apps. Personalization algorithms help us choose the optimal products to buy on Amazon, the best movies to watch on Netflix, the ideal person to date through Tinder and Match.com, the most useful contacts on LinkedIn, and the most compelling posts and articles to read on Facebook. But in our imagining, we generally nod politely at these recommendations and make our own choices. After all, we are in charge here.

And yet consider these facts: 80 percent of viewing hours streamed on Netflix originate from automated recommendations. By some estimates nearly 35 percent of sales at Amazon originate from automated recommendations. And the vast majority of matches on dating apps such as Tinder and OkCupid are initiated by algorithms. Given these numbers, many of us clearly do not have quite the freedom of choice that we believe we do.

One reason is that products are often designed in ways that make us act impulsively and against our better judgment. For example, suppose you have a big meeting at work tomorrow. Ideally, you want to spend some time preparing for it in the evening and then get a good night's rest. But before you can do either, a notification pops up on your phone indicating that a friend tagged you on Facebook. *This will take a minute*, you tell yourself as you click on it. But after logging in you discover a long feed of posts by friends. A few clicks later you find yourself watching a YouTube video that one of them shared. As soon as the video ends, YouTube suggests other related and interesting videos. Before you know it, it's 1:00 a.m., and it's clear that you will need an all-nighter to get ready for the following morning's meeting. This has happened to most of us. The reason this behavior is so common, as some product designers have noted, is that popular design approaches—such as the use of notifications and gamification to increase user engagement—exploit and amplify human vulnerabilities, such as our need for social approval, or our inability to resist immediate gratification even when we recognize that it comes with long-term costs. While we might feel as if we are making our own choices, we're often nudged or even tricked into making them.

Another reason that we aren't truly in control of our choices is that when we search for a hotel on Expedia, browse online dating profiles, or shop for a book, we're seeing only a small fraction of all the potentially relevant information available. Although we experience a clear sense of free will by making the final decision regarding what we see, read, or buy, the fact is that 99 percent of all possible alternatives were excluded.

You probably don't mind saving all the time you might have wasted in sifting through inferior options to arrive at a final choice. But algorithms do not simply help us find products or information more quickly that we might have found eventually without their assistance. In truth, they exert a significant influence on precisely what and how much we consume.

Consider the role of search algorithms. Given millions of possible search results, thousands of which are likely to be highly relevant to a particular query, Google's algorithms determine which ones are featured at the very top of the results page. This ranking exerts a powerful influence on our responses. About 33 percent of clicks go to the number-one result in Google searches; fewer than 10 percent go to links outside of the top ten results.

Automated recommendations are also a major driver of choice online. More than any individual or organization—including Oprah, the National Book Awards, or *The New York Times*—Amazon's recommendation algorithms have the biggest influence on which books people are reading. Automated recommendations drive purchase decisions across a wide variety of product categories, from kitchenware and perfumes to electronics and artwork. Beyond retailers such as Amazon and Walmart .com, online media companies such as Netflix, Spotify, Apple's iTunes, and Google's YouTube all employ algorithmic recommendations to gently nudge us in specific directions.

The impact of algorithms are also experienced on social media websites, where we are likely to believe that our friends are the chief drivers of the content we see. In reality, algorithms play an equally important role. Every time a user opens Facebook's app or website, there are on average about 1,500 potential stories or posts that Facebook can show. Its algorithms determine which ones you should read first, which can be read later, and even which you don't need to read at all. The algorithms consider a number of factors to determine the posts they show us—how often we interact with the friend who posted; the number of likes, comments, and shares that the post received in aggregate and from our friends; how recently the post appeared; whether any users tried to hide it; and so on. Instagram and Twitter have also recently adopted algorithmic feeds. Given how social networks have become the gateway for online news and media discovery for so many of us, news-feed algorithms are crucial to determining the reportage we read and the opinions we form about the world around us.

Perhaps inevitably, algorithms are not just selecting the media we see on social networks but are also silently determining the network itself—that is, whom we allow into our personal and professional lives. LinkedIn's algorithms will magically remind you of the people you met last week or emailed yesterday so they can be added to your professional network. Interested in reconnecting with childhood friends? Facebook's algorithms will recommend whom to add as friends on Facebook. And why stop at friends? Algorithms built by companies such as Tinder, Match.com, and eHarmony will even determine whom you date or marry. Algorithms are the primary drivers of matches on on-line dating apps and websites, which, by some estimates, are used by as much as 40 percent of the singles population in the United States.

───

Opinions are one force in determining the actions we take as individuals; our feelings are another. Consider the case of Match .com, launched in 1995 and now the country's most popular dating website.

Gary Kremen, the man who conceived of Match.com, was inspired in part by newspaper classified ads. If you're old enough, you might remember that placing a personal ad usually involved giving a few details about yourself and a few about the person you were looking to meet: "Single male, 35, avid reader, seeks single female, 20–30, fit and fun." The job of finding a match was left to the reader of the ad. Match.com's earliest algorithms sought to replicate this model, but also to step in as the actual matchmaker, noticing the single male whom the busy single woman might have missed and putting the two in touch.

Take the simple ability to link supply and demand, automate it, provide the scale the internet allows, and you have a winning business. Indeed, Match.com and its many competitors have attracted millions of paying subscribers, if also the scorn of a segment of the public that views even old-fashioned newspaper personal ads with suspicion. But for all the public outcry about safety issues, anonymity, and the degree to which these ads have promoted a hook-up culture, no one questioned that they were simply giving their users exactly what they wanted.

Except they weren't—at least not in the most literal sense. In 2011 Match opened its doors to a *Financial Times* reporter, David Gelles, who learned that the company found it best to ignore, at least partially, what users said they wanted. Although the company's algorithms asked users to define their ideal partners, people with those characteristics weren't the ones Match urged them to reach out to. Rather, the website would send daily recommendations that weren't based on what users had said they wanted, but on something else entirely: the profiles the users had visited.

"Before, matches were based on the criteria you set. You meet her criteria, and she meets yours, so you're a good match," said Amarnath Thombre, a senior vice-president for strategy and analytics at the time, and now chief executive officer there—as well as a board member for another dating app, Tinder. "But when we researched the data . . . [we found] people were doing something very different from the things they said they wanted on their profile."

When Match's algorithms began sending recommendations to users based on where they clicked rather than what they typed, the process seemed to work: political conservatives who'd been lurking on the profiles of liberals got pushed into finally saying "hello"; Catholic girls who thought they wanted to find a match within their religion were instead meeting, and falling for, Jewish men; and men insisting they wanted a blonde were finding love anyway when the algorithm introduced them to brunettes. Curiously, Match's analytics team found that conservatives were more open to contacting a liberal than vice-versa; Catholic women were especially unlikely to message a Hindu or atheist male; and men were very particular about the hair color of a potential partner.

"We are so focused on behavior rather than stated preferences because we find people break from their stated preferences so often," Thombre explained to Gelles.

Match was, and is, trying to maximize the chances that its users find, in the broadest sense, what they're looking for. But the decision to ignore their stated preferences, even if this violates the implicit contract between the user and the algorithm, raises many questions. If our actions contradict our words, shouldn't *we* get to decide which of the two determines the course of something as intimate as our love lives? Is this a case of algorithms serving our desires or manipulating them? The answer may be debatable. But what isn't debatable is that the approach works. Gelles reported that more than half the initial messages sent by suitors on Match.com originate from algorithmic recommendations. And other online companies are following suit. Today, many algorithms have stopped asking users what they want. Instead, they lurk behind the scenes and try to infer it.

Look around you and ask what drives your product, media, and people choices. Unless you are a tech Luddite, algorithms are silently rearranging your life. The conventional narrative is that algorithms will make faster and better decisions for all of us, leaving us with more time for family and leisure. But the reality isn't so simple. In this brave new world many of our choices are in fact predestined, and all the seemingly small effects that algorithms have on our decisions add up to a transformative impact on our lives. Because who we are, ultimately, is the sum total of the various decisions we make over a lifetime.

In 2012 Facebook conducted a study in which they tweaked their news-feed algorithm to show some users more "hard news"—think more "war in Iraq" and less "cats fitting in boxes." They then measured how many of these users clicked the "I voted" button that most of us saw at the top of our Facebook feed in November 2012. They compared the self-reported voter turnout of this group against a control group whose news-feed algorithm had not been modified. The researchers found that users who had their news-feed algorithm tweaked increased their voting turnout by three percentage points, from 64 percent for the control group to 67 percent for the treatment group. A follow-up survey found that these users were also significantly more likely to report that they paid attention to the government. Three percentage points might not sound like much, but the outcomes of elections, including the U.S. presidential election in 2016, are frequently determined by smaller amounts.*†

Similarly, in January 2012, researchers at Facebook ran a study to investigate whether and how emotions spread socially. They selected 689,003 users and assigned them to one of two experiments. In the first, the news-feed algorithm for some users was modified such that some positive posts were randomly removed from their news feed. In effect, they were seeing less positivity in their online world. In the second experiment, some negative posts were randomly removed from news feeds. In each experiment, there was a comparable group of control users whose feeds were not biased toward either positive or negative

---

*Some Facebook users might feel uncomfortable about this experiment. It would certainly be alarming if Facebook were intentionally encouraging particular people to vote for a particular cause. However, that is not what happened in this study. Rather, researchers were simply trying to understand how different types of algorithms can affect social behavior. That said, the study raises many questions about ethics in the design of algorithms. If Facebook deploys the "hard news" version of their algorithm, does that mean they are manipulating people into voting? What about the choice to not deploy the "hard news" algorithm? Would that mean Facebook is manipulating people into *not* voting? Even if all Facebook is doing is to encourage all of its users to vote, can that affect election results? Women, younger people, and urban dwellers—all of whom were more likely to support Obama than Romney in 2012—are more-active Facebook users, suggesting that the scientific experiment might have favored Democrats. It's not completely clear who benefits from either version, but what is clear is that algorithms wield immense power, and we should be attentive to how they impact social outcomes. That is a theme I will return to later in this book.
†The Facebook fake news controversy that erupted soon after the November 2016 U.S. presidential election is a far more alarming example of manipulation, albeit not entirely algorithmic. More on that in the next chapter.

posts. The study then evaluated the tone of the posts written by the users whose news feeds were significantly altered against the corresponding control group.

The researchers found that emotion was contagious: people who saw fewer negative posts were more positive in their own posts, while those who saw fewer positive posts became more negative in theirs. Although the study intended to demonstrate that emotions expressed by our online friends influence our mood, the findings make an equally important statement about the potential impact of automated algorithms that select the media we see. If you felt energized and ready to take on the world yesterday and feel despondent and hopeless today, it may very well be related to the social media posts selected by your news-feed algorithm.*

Tai wasn't wrong to feel uneasy about the chart he drew, as it illustrated well the fact that the sense of free will he experienced when he made the relevant choices was at least partially an illusion. When we spoke after class that afternoon, I shared the Facebook studies with Tai. He responded by relating how he had spent his college years learning to make his own decisions and

---

*Not surprisingly, the study caused intense outrage. Protocols for research using human subjects call for getting explicit consent from participants. Facebook did not get consent from its participants, arguing instead that users give blanket consent to such testing under its terms of service. The actual impact of the study on users' emotions was probably minimal—users who saw less positivity in their news feed on average wrote one fewer positive word per thousand words in their subsequent posts. But the PR damage was done and the study resulted in a media storm. Eventually, the study's lead researcher issued an apology.

take responsibility for them. He had felt in charge. But now he was coming to realize that the obstacles he believed stood in the way of his freedom in thinking and acting were not other people, but the digital tools he used to simplify day-to-day decisions. "Wow, to think that most choices I make are not my own," Tai, a youngster who had clearly never been married, muttered.

I understood Tai's sense of disbelief. After all, losing our sense of free will is no small matter. But I didn't offer him any assurances. Instead, I told him that this may just be the tip of the iceberg.

2.

The Law of Unanticipated Consequences

> In theory, there is no difference between theory and practice, while in practice, there is.
>
> Benjamin Brewster

S itting on a crowded commuter bus one morning in the late spring of 2004, Kevin Gibbs, then in his mid-twenties, was rethinking his decision to live in San Francisco. After graduating from Stanford a few years earlier, he had been eager to embrace the excitement of city life—as opposed to the suburban sprawl of Silicon Valley, where he now worked as a software engineer for Google. He had been hired to help optimize the company's massive data center—the network of IT equipment that stores data and powers Google searches worldwide. Most of this had to be done on-site, and what little he could tackle remotely required a stable internet connection. But a few weeks into that job, he realized that the one perk of the commute on the company bus—that he could use the traveling time productively—was negated by the fact that he could not get a steady enough signal. So he decided to take on a project for fun.

Inching along busy Route 101, he started writing code. The first thing he programmed was a URL predictor that would guess what a user was typing in the address bar and autocomplete it. For example, if someone entered "www.n," www.nytimes.com would appear, as the code examined the data to see where most users who had started typing this URL ended. If a user added an "e"—"www.ne"—the code would suggest www.netflix.com instead.

A coworker sitting next to Gibbs on the bus noticed what he was up to and asked, "What if you did it for search terms?" The idea made sense, and soon Gibbs had built the first version of Google's autocomplete tool. As with the URL predictor, it attempted to predict what you would type—but this time aimed to predict the words and phrases you might type in Google's search bar. He based the predictions on the user's own recent search queries, on trending news stories, and on what other people were searching for on Google. The tool saved users time; even only a few seconds per search query add up, given that many of us type hundreds of queries a day. At its best, it also helped scattered, distracted users sharpen their focus by making relevant suggestions.

The tool was launched in December of 2004, but as an optional add-on that was largely overlooked by the average user, and it stayed that way for another four years. But autocomplete slowly started gaining the attention of more people, some of whom set it as their homepage. Marissa Mayer, then a prominent Google executive (and later Yahoo's CEO), showed sufficient interest in the tool that Google eventually staffed a team and launched autocomplete as a default feature on its search engine in 2008.

Today it's a great time-saving feature in a search engine that is already making our personal and professional lives more efficient. In addition, it adds a soupçon of fun to an otherwise routine search experience. Even if the autocomplete suggestions are completely unrelated to my query, I'll sometimes take a look at them, because they offer a revealing window into what's on other people's minds. Type in "Never put a," and you will see suggestions such as "Never put a sock in a toaster"; the top suggestion for "Can I vacuum" is "my dog." "After the launch, I realized that people would sit down on the web browser and type what was on their mind and not really think whether a search engine could answer that. They had an expectation that they could say anything on their mind and see what themes came up," Gibbs told me during a recent conversation. There is even a website called Google Feud which offers an online game modeled on the TV show *Family Feud*, except that contestants guess which suggestions autocomplete has made to a particular query. And surveys say the game is a hit. It's been played by nearly 30 million users and referenced on multiple TV shows.

Gibbs views his brilliant addition to the Google search experience as an almost inevitable outcome. "I'm sure it would have happened if I hadn't done it," he told a tech reporter for the website *All Things D* in 2013. "I think it's one of those history of invention things—where there was one guy who developed it in Germany and one guy in Russia, and it turns out they were doing it in the same year. I haven't found my guy, but I think it was just an idea that was just so ripe to have happened."

Today, most of us take the autocomplete algorithm so much for granted that we scarcely notice the feature when we use Google. But however well it increases efficiency, its use can also have unanticipated consequences. In December 2016 writer Carole Cadwalladr typed the two innocuous words "are jews" into Google's search box. It responded with "are jews a race" as its first guess, followed by "are jews white" and "are jews christian." Each of these guesses would be bound to inspire some interesting discussions, but it was the fourth guess that caught Cadwalladr's attention: "are jews evil." Upon selecting the suggestion, she was led to search results featuring neo-Nazi websites and links to anti-Semitic YouTube videos. She was shocked that Google not only made it so easy to access such hateful content but even directed users there.

Cadwalladr hadn't stumbled upon one freak case. A series of ads by U.N. Women (a United Nations organization promoting female equality and empowerment) is based entirely around autocomplete suggestions: the ads reveal that typing in "women should" leads to "women should stay at home" and "women should be slaves." Similarly, "women shouldn't" leads to "women shouldn't have rights" and "women shouldn't vote." I can't look at these autocomplete suggestions without wondering whether the correct suggestion should actually be "women should be seeing better days in the twenty-first century."

Pick any subject around which prejudice exists, and autocomplete reveals it. At one level, it is useful to know that so many people are typing in such queries. It's hard to solve a problem until people begin to understand how deep and pervasive it is. But it's far more disturbing to ask if Google might have unintentionally led impressionable people who did not initially seek this information to webpages filled with biased and prejudiced commentaries, effectively delivering new audiences directly to hate-mongering sites.*

Gibbs recognizes that the tool he invented might be shaping people's attitudes and behaviors by directing them to certain content and effectively censoring other content. "In my mind, the social shift is important," he said. "This was a side project, but then it got serious." But he also points out just how hard it is to strike the right balance: "How do you choose what's important and what's not? And it has to be based on an objective standard, not my own opinion." As an example, Gibbs cites the challenge in ensuring that the algorithm steers away from suggesting pornography but, at the same time, does not censor sexuality. That distinction between the two may be clear to us,

---

*Google's support website allows users to report offensive autocompletes. The company has been quick to react to and remove offensive suggestions once they are notified of them. Although Google has acted responsibly, the question remains how it can best prevent such issues rather than simply react to them.

even if we don't always agree on the parameters, but it's much harder to teach an algorithm U.S. Supreme Court Justice Potter Stewart's famous "I know it when I see it" formula. Similarly, Gibbs found that although it was easy to add a blacklist of obscenities, it was a lot more challenging as a coder to ensure that the system did not suggest anything that was hateful.

The gender and racial bias of Google's autocomplete is by no means an exception in the world of algorithms. Recently a group of technologists launched the world's first beauty contest judged by AI. The idea was to use objective factors such as facial symmetry to make choices free from human biases and errors. The scientists used advanced machine learning techniques and a large dataset of pre-labeled photos to create their beauty assessment algorithm. Although more than 6,000 people from 100 countries participated, the 44 winners chosen by the software were nearly all white, with a few from East Asia. Only one of the finalists had dark skin, even though there were many contestants from Africa and India. The scientists who helped build the algorithms acknowledged that their AI judge had a bias against dark skin.

Google Photos faced a similar issue in 2015 with its photo-tagging algorithm. Jacky Alciné, a software engineer and an activist focused on issues of race and diversity in the tech world, wasn't looking for a cause when he sat down one evening in Oakland, California, to organize photos that had been collecting on his phone for months. As he started flipping through the images using the Google Photos app, however, something caught his eye. Amid pictures labeled "Bikes," "Cars," and "Graduation" by Google's auto-tagging tool, one photo—of Jacky and a friend grinning happily into the camera—had been auto-tagged "Gorillas." This was not just strange, but offensive, given that both individuals were black. He took to Twitter and posted a screenshot, which was retweeted more than 3,000 times within a few days.

Google quickly apologized and explained that a tool millions of people appreciated and relied on as a time-saving essential was also, unfortunately, racist. Or to put it more kindly—and accurately—racially confused. Image-processing algorithms that hadn't been trained on a large enough number of photos of black people were unable to account for different skin tones and lighting. Google's quick reaction kept the bug from becoming a public relations mess, and most Twitter users reacted with humor or curiosity rather than anger. But the problem was far from unique.

———

The concept of *unanticipated consequences* isn't uniquely applicable to decisions made by algorithms. The term was used by economists such as Adam Smith as early as the 1700s, but it was popularized in the twentieth century by American sociologist Robert Merton, who applied it to unexpected side effects of decisions made by humans. The literature documents three different types of unanticipated consequences: *unforeseen benefits*, *perverse results*, and *unexpected drawbacks*. Unforeseen benefits are, by definition, serendipitous. Famously, the drug Viagra was developed to lower blood pressure, but its role was "elevated" when it had the unexpected side effect of tumescence in men during clinical trials. Although unexpected benefits are relevant to algorithmic decisions, they are rarely the subject of much controversy or debate, and so are not a topic I will discuss in detail in this book.

Perverse results refer to situations in which an intervention worsens precisely the outcome it was meant to improve. One well-known example is the so-called "cobra effect," which played out in colonial India. Legend has it that a British government officer in Delhi wanted to address what he perceived to be the menace of cobras in India's capital, so he announced a bounty for every dead snake that was presented to authorities. Initially, this produced good results. However, a few enterprising individuals soon realized that it was easier to farm a cobra and produce its head than to catch one in the wild. When the government recognized that this was going on, the scheme was canceled. In response, the cobra farmers, who now had no possible use for the snakes, freed them. The result was an increase in Delhi's cobra population.*

---

*Back when I was sixteen, my parents moved to a less inhabited part of Bengaluru, a thriving city in South India sometimes referred to as India's Silicon Valley. Although the city was already getting crowded, land was more abundant and housing cheaper in this part of the city. But it also meant lots of wild meadows nearby, an ideal environment for snakes. As I was walking into the house one day, I saw what looked like a snake slither away into the pots in my mom's garden. Thinking it unlikely that I had actually seen one, I started inspecting the pots one by one until I was confronted by a cobra. To my surprise, the snake seemed to be more frightened of me than I was of it. I considered letting it be in the hope that it'd return to

Unexpected drawbacks refer to unanticipated negative outcomes that happen *in addition to* the desired positive result. They arise in many settings. One occurred in the northeast of England, in an industrial town whose recorded history dates at least as far back as the *Domesday Book*, a survey of England commissioned by William the Conqueror and completed in 1086. Back then, it consisted of twenty-one households and was known by its old Norse name, *Escumetorp*; on modern maps, it's called Scunthorpe. When a Scunthorpe resident named David Blackie entered the name of the town when setting up an AOL account in 1996, his registration was blocked, and no reason was given. The people on AOL's helpline guessed at first that their algorithms had balked at the surname "Blackie," marking it as a racial slur. But the trouble turned out to be the name "Scunthorpe," whose embedded "c word" got the machines blushing.

AOL's attempt to block offensive language usually worked. But it also happened to block at least one patently inoffensive name. The solution? AOL users were told temporarily to spell Scunthorpe "Sconthorpe." A spokeswoman assured the local newspaper that technicians were working to remove the block. Until then, she said—neatly conflating the software's intended

---

where it came from. Instead, I thought it better to catch it and release it in a safer area. I asked a neighbor to help, and he recruited a local construction worker. Much as the construction guy tried, the snake was too fearful to leave the pots and work its way around the compound wall toward the meadows. Eventually, the worker insisted that the snake had seen his face and would return in the night to bite him. Much to my chagrin, he killed the cobra. My goal had been to help release it to the open fields, but a perverse result thwarted my plan.

effect and unexpected drawback—"we have renamed the town in order not to cause offence."

———

In the summer of 2005 Nathaniel "Nate" Stevens, a sophomore at Penn, decided to forgo a summer internship to help his father out at the family car dealership. He had worked there before, processing paperwork and talking to potential customers, but now, armed with some marketing skills, he decided to tackle the business's approach to advertising. At the time, consumers were beginning to use Google in growing numbers to find local services. If you lived in Connecticut and were looking for a Toyota dealer, you simply Googled "Connecticut Toyota dealer." Yet while buyers had taken to the web, local businesses were still stuck with hoping customers would look for them in a fat yellow book. Nate knew that within a few years the Yellow Pages would go the way of the dodo and the Macarena. He decided to pull his dad's dealership into the twenty-first century, placed ads for the business on Google, and soon discovered the enormous untapped potential that the web offered.

The archetypal local business is a mom-and-pop affair: it's not tech savvy and doesn't have a large marketing team to figure out how to advertise on Google. The process of doing so was not as simple as cutting a check to a Yellow Pages company and asking for a half-page ad. Instead, Google ran live auctions to sell the limited ad space available on its search results pages. For a small business, this required figuring out what kinds of search terms consumers might type into a search engine and how to bid for each term. Sensing an opportunity, Nate started a company to help local business owners, such as dentists, gardeners, and realtors, advertise on Google. Initially, he made the key decisions—which search terms or keywords consumers might be typing in, and how much to bid for each—on behalf of his clients, but he soon realized that this was neither cost-effective nor scalable. Nor was there any way he could hire and train enough people to serve the hundreds of thousands of small businesses that might be looking for just this sort of help.

I learned about Nate's dilemma when he called me to discuss how to build an algorithm to automate these decisions. I decided to try an approach that started with an informed guess but improved each day, as new data emerged on the number of searches, clicks, and "leads"—potential customers who went on to contact the business in question—obtained for a given search term. A dentist in Washington, D.C., for example, might consider bidding on "Washington DC dentist," "DC teeth lumineers," and "dental fillings," among thousands of possible search terms. Over time, the algorithm would slowly move the ad budget away from poorly performing keywords and toward the better-performing ones. Within a month, the algorithm would, in theory, be able to make better decisions about search terms and auction bids than a human counterpart could.

During the initial weeks of testing, the algorithm produced very odd, potentially ruinous suggestions (e.g., a bid of $10,000 per click for one keyword, where a human would rarely go over $20). But after several iterations, the bids were finally making sense and producing good results: lowering costs for our clients and delivering more customers to them.

We declared our project a success, which is never a good idea. Soon after, a strange puzzle arose, as our clients' cost of advertising began skyrocketing. Where an advertiser previously got fifty leads from an ad budget of $2,000, she was now seeing half that number. This did not happen across the board; performance dipped for some advertisers but remained strong for others. As I sifted through the results, another puzzle emerged. The more clients we had in any given market—in effect, the more data we had available—the poorer the performance. For example, six out of ten advertisers who showed up on the first page of the query "DC dentist" were our clients. And performance had deteriorated for all of them. But for a single caterer in Philly, the algorithm continued delivering exceptional results.

Analysis eventually revealed the reasons for the perverse result: all six dentists in Washington were using precisely the same algorithm, which identified the same set of "highly valuable keywords" for these clients. Each therefore bid aggressively to secure a top position for those keywords, but only Google would emerge better off in such a bidding war. Was our business idea kaput? Fortunately not. If the same algorithm and the same underlying data drove advertising strategies for all clients, a regional bidding war for terms deemed valuable would be inevitable. But in the real world, different firms have different specialties.

One dentist might excel at teeth whitening and prefer that to be his primary search term, while another might want to emphasize her expertise at dental extraction. They might even serve different customer demographics, e.g., children or the elderly, insured patients or those paying out of pocket. To fix our algorithm, we needed to modify it so that it took into account each advertiser's data to identify the search terms that were uniquely valuable to that business. Once we did so, we stopped the vicious feedback loop that was causing everyone to chase the same keywords.* Our fine-tuned algorithms became the basis of a company we later named Yodle, and eventually helped to power the advertising decisions of more than 50,000 small businesses.

Perverse results such as the one created by our algorithm usually come as a surprise. But thanks to a cycle of testing and

---

*It's often easier to reprogram an algorithm than the human mind. A friend's father started selling used books on Amazon a few years ago and developed a policy of matching whatever the lowest price was for a given product. If a "Used—Very Good" copy of Barack Obama's *Dreams from My Father* was selling for $4.99, Fred would post his copy at that price, too. After a while, he noticed one seller would consistently lower his price once Fred matched it—by one cent. Fred would dutifully match again at the lower price, and the next day find that his competitor had lowered his asking price by another cent. Frustrated, Fred engaged in what the U.S. Department of Justice might justifiably call collusion: he wrote to his rival seller pointing out that if this pattern continued, they would both wind up at a final price of $.01. The seller wrote back saying that he had a long and successful track record as an Amazon seller, and had no intention of changing his ways. Nor, he said, could Fred count on predicting his next, savvy move. He concluded: "Sometimes I match and sometimes I beat." After the exchange, he continued beating. Fred stopped matching; the old hand had won the battle. As for Fred, he was glad he hadn't automated his pricing strategy.

refining that is routine at all tech firms, they are often quickly detected and resolved. Unexpected drawbacks can prove trickier.

Consider what Facebook experienced in the summer of 2016. The site's Trending Topics section, which was managed by human editors, was accused of having a liberal bias. A former employee revealed that news stories from conservative sources were suppressed by the editors, even though they were trending among users. Furthermore, some "news curators," as Facebook called these editors, were told to insert certain stories from liberal sources, even if those stories weren't actually trending. The leak caused significant embarrassment at Facebook, but the senior management acted quickly to address the issue. The obvious solution to a problem related to human bias—particularly when the challenge was merely a matter of tallying the numbers of "views" and "shares" a particular post receives—was to replace humans with an algorithm that selected trending news stories. An algorithm, after all, could not be accused of having a political agenda.

The result is well known by now: The Trending Topics algorithm failed to question the credibility of sources and inadvertently promoted "fake news." The result was that inaccurate and often fabricated stories were widely circulated in the months leading up to the U.S. presidential election. According to one estimate, the top twenty false stories in that period received greater engagement on Facebook than the top twenty legitimate ones.

How could Facebook, with its massive resources and army

of talented engineers, have deployed an algorithm that was so flawed? How was it that the unanticipated consequence at Yodle—essentially a two-man algorithm team at the time—was detected almost as soon as it started playing up, but that the one at Facebook went undetected until it was, arguably, too late?

These two experiences reveal an interesting difference between perverse results and unintended drawbacks. Perverse results are associated with a deterioration of exactly the situation you are trying to improve. They may be unanticipated because the algorithms are deployed in complex systems. How people respond to a cobra bounty, for example, may be simply too difficult to predict beforehand. How the bidding decisions of different advertisers interact may similarly be too complex to anticipate. But because they affect precisely what is measured, they have a better chance of being detected.

In contrast, unintended drawbacks affect outcomes or situations other than the one you are trying to improve. But how can we detect them when there are just too many potential outcomes to plan for? Facebook's engineers probably measured carefully the political slant of their algorithm, given that it was developed in response to the political bias of human editors. They may have ensured that the highlighted stories were genuinely popular, given that the goal of the algorithm was to feature trending items. But they apparently did not take into account the possibility of some stories being false.

Unexpected drawbacks and perverse results are both, by definition, unexpected. But unlike perverse results, unexpected drawbacks don't affect the exact performance metric data scientists are tracking. As such, it may be impossible to completely avoid them.

———

Promotion of hateful content by Google's autocomplete algorithm. Racist tagging of photos. Racism in sentencing algorithms used in courts. The spread of fake news by news curation algorithms. Such events are becoming increasingly common in a world where algorithms are making ever more of our important decisions for us.

To understand the implications of unanticipated consequences of algorithms, consider this analogy: suppose you have a frequently recurring headache, and your doctor gives you a medication that is guaranteed to cure it within two weeks. Who would choose not to take such a powerful drug? What if you were told that the pill also causes an itch that disappears once you stop the medication? The answer would still be "yes" for almost all of us. What if it caused long-term memory loss in 1 out of every 10,000 patients? Perhaps that small a risk is one you are willing to take. What if there's a 5 percent chance of significant loss of memory? What if there's a 5 percent chance of memory loss and an even higher chance of seizures? At what point does the cure become worse than the disease?

Data-driven algorithms that direct our decision making are much like the medication in the example above. They may do an exceptional job of achieving what they are designed to achieve. But they also have side effects. Much of our focus, both as users of these algorithms and as their designers, is on a single, immediate aspect of their performance: "Will the pill fix the headache?" Asking only that question leaves aside any consideration of possible side effects. In fact, we are not even aware of what they might be; algorithmic suggestions don't come with a warning label. Maybe it's time they did.

Gibbs, the inventor of Google's autocomplete, believes that companies should disclose more details about their algorithms, though he acknowledges that even this may not be sufficient. "You have to raise awareness and understanding of it, and that's where we will hopefully end up as the years go on. I think we should be rightfully . . . suspicious is the wrong word . . . we should think critically about them. If there is an algorithm that can influence behavior, we'd want to understand why and how that works. That's where we should reach for all these algorithms that influence our lives and behaviors."

I believe that's an important goal. So let's move on to discuss it in Part Two.

ALGORITHMIC THINKING

3.

Omelet Recipes for Computers

HOW ALGORITHMS ARE PROGRAMMED

> For me, great algorithms are the poetry of computation. Just like verse, they can be terse, allusive, dense, and even mysterious. But once unlocked, they cast a brilliant new light on some aspect of computing.
>
> Francis Sullivan, computer scientist, *The Joy of Algorithms*

n November 2003 the American publisher Houghton Mifflin took a gamble on a new writer from England named Jon Mc-Gregor. He had attracted the attention of critics in the United Kingdom for being the youngest longlisted author for the prestigious Man Booker Prize the previous year, and now Houghton was hoping to leverage that distinction into a successful print run for his novel in the States.

The odds of commercial success for McGregor's book, *If*

Nobody Speaks of Remarkable Things, weren't particularly high. The novel told the story of the inhabitants of one street in an anonymous English city, celebrating, according to his publishers, "the flotsam and jetsam of everyday life." Quiet novels about people's everyday existences are generally a hard sell; McGregor's was rich in cups of tea and neighborhood cricket—hardly familiar territory for the average American reader.*

The novel's Amazon sales rank in December 2003, a month after its American release, was 8,535, and it had received only two reader reviews. As time passed, even as other literary honors rolled in, demand for the book remained low; by the following March, its Amazon position had fallen to 25,397.

And then, suddenly, sales started picking up. *If Nobody Speaks of Remarkable Things* never reached bestseller status, but it did rise up the ranks, reaching 2,102 in May 2004.

What explained the sudden interest in McGregor's book six

---

*I know, firsthand, the challenge of engaging Americans in stories of cricket. Having grown up in India where cricket is almost a religion, I tend to pepper my lectures with references to the sport. Unlike McGregor, I have a trick to bait my students into those stories. I usually begin with: "I realize that not many of you know about cricket. One way to understand its rules is by comparing it to its poorer and less creative cousin called baseball." That gets the attention of the baseball fans even if it makes them a bit combative. A student once asked, to everyone's amusement, "Is cricket the fast-paced sport that takes five days for a game to finish?" I responded: "Yes, it is indeed so interesting that you can be hooked on a game for five days in a row." Between you and me, I will reveal that an English politician once said that cricket is "a game which the English, not being a spiritual people, have invented in order to give themselves some conception of eternity." But don't share this with my students.

months after it was published? Little in world events that spring would have drawn Americans' attention to a book about everyday English life: The news was focused on the 9/11 Commission in Washington, prisoner abuse at Abu Ghraib, and attempts at postwar reconstruction in Iraq. Oprah Winfrey had picked the 1940 classic *The Heart Is a Lonely Hunter* as her book club's next read. The Pulitzer Prize for fiction was awarded in early April—but the winner, *The Known World* by Edward P. Jones, was a historical novel about black slave owners. None of this seemed to explain the sudden interest in *If Nobody Speaks of Remarkable Things*.

The reason, as you may have guessed by now, stems from the way algorithms work.

If you're writing a recipe for a plain omelet, whether you call for greasing the pan with butter or coconut oil will make a difference in how the omelet will taste. Algorithms are no different. When programmers develop them, they make many design choices that have "downstream" consequences on our decisions that are hard to anticipate. The complexity comes, of course, from the fact that we're not merely making omelets.

Consider recommendation algorithms—the ones that suggest movies on Netflix, contacts on LinkedIn, and books on Amazon. In this chapter, I will explain the inner workings of these algorithms and how they come up with those often quirky—and sometimes brilliant—recommendations, and how simple design choices can have unintended (and complex) results.

———

It's Spring Break—a rare week on campus without meetings, which gives me time to get some writing done. I open Spotify and play my "All-time Faves" playlist. It will run in the background over the next few hours while I make progress on this book. I have typed only a few lines when I sense that the music is bothering me. Even though it's been weeks since I logged into Spotify, I have begun to notice just how familiar all the tracks sound. These are mostly songs from the '90s that I have been listening to for more than twenty years. I suppose even "All-time Faves" have a shelf life. I wonder if my YouTube playlists or Pandora stations will be better. A few minutes into each of them and I realize that every single playlist of mine is dominated by songs from my high school and college years. I am musically stuck in the '90s.

Because I'm professionally in a good position to be aware of the algorithmic solution to old-fogeyism, I decide the writing can wait, while I test out—in the name of research, of course, not procrastination—the recommendation engines on three digital music platforms: Pandora, Last.fm, and Spotify. I haven't made these choices at random. Each system represents a very different approach, modeled on how we as humans might make a recommendation. For example, if you asked me for advice on music, and I knew you liked "Yellow" by Coldplay, I might try to think of other songs that were acoustically similar to it. Pandora's algorithms are based on this method, known as "content-based recommendation." These systems start with detailed information about a product's characteristics and then search for other products with similar qualities. If I knew you liked "Yellow" but I wasn't really familiar with Coldplay's music, I might try instead to think of someone I knew who also likes Coldplay and ask her what else she listens to. Last.fm uses this second approach, known as "collaborative filtering." Spotify tries to combine these two methods.

I know the theory underlying each platform, but how might my experiment play out in practice? I start with Pandora and ask it to recommend music based on my interest in "Thunder" by Imagine Dragons, one of my rare recent discoveries. Pandora serves up "Ride" by the band Twenty One Pilots. It informs me that the song was recommended because it features "a dub production, a reggae feel, acoustic rhythm piano, use of a string ensemble and major key tonality." The description sounds convincing enough, and my ears approve. It's not technically a new discovery—I've heard this track before—but this is the first time I register the name of the song or the artist. The next recommendation is "Weak" by AJR which, Pandora notes, features "similar electronica influences, mild rhythmic syncopation, acoustic rhythm piano, extensive vamping, and major key tonality." As you can see, Pandora has a deep understanding of music and the vocabulary to articulate it. Its online radio service emerged from the Music Genome Project, in which musicologists listened to individual tracks and assigned more than 450 attributes to each. These range from the obvious, such as the extent of instrumentation in the music, to the esoteric, such as "rhythmic syncopation." Once you indicate that you like a song on Pandora, the algorithm finds other songs that have similar musical qualities.

The first eleven recommendations from Pandora all sound acoustically very similar to "Thunder," especially "Young Dumb & Broke" by Khalid. They all win my approval. The twelfth track, "Sail" by AWOLNATION, is okay. Should I give it a thumbs up or down (Pandora's rating system) or just not rate it? I decide aggressive choices can better guide the algorithm and go with a thumbs down. Pandora now decides to take a dramatic turn and begins playing songs with significant electronica influences. The first two tracks are fine, but I really dislike "All Time Low" by Jon Bellion. Another thumbs down, this time without hesitation, and again the algorithm adapts. I listen to twenty songs in total, fourteen of which are completely new to me. The six familiar selections aren't ones I would have searched for myself, but I like most of the music. Pandora's algorithms also tell me that I apparently like songs with "extensive vamping." I am not sure what that means, exactly, but the next time I'm at a live show, I'll shout out a request for more vamping. It can't hurt, right?

To try a very different musical genre, I ask Pandora to create a custom station based on my interest in "Pashmina," a song from a Bollywood movie composed by musician Amit Trivedi. I listen to the twenty songs it selects, which it informs me feature emotional vocals and simple harmonic progressions. I find the tracks actually to be quite different from one another and suspect the fact that they are all Indian film music dominates other qualifiers for Pandora.

Pandora's approach worked for me, but only because someone had taken the time to catalogue detailed attributes of all its offerings. Collecting such data manually is incredibly time-consuming and expensive.

I turn to Last.fm's recommendations. Out of the twenty tracks it suggests in response to my entry of "Thunder," I am familiar with only five. Acoustically speaking, some of the songs (like "Magic" by Coldplay) sound very different from "Thunder," because the collaborative filtering approach used by Last .fm is based on the "People who bought this also bought . . ." and "People like you also liked . . ." recommendations that we often see on Amazon and other websites. While this enhances discovery of a wider range of music, it comes at a cost. While I truly disliked only one of Pandora's recommendations, I dislike about six of Last.fm's recommendations. Moreover, unlike Pandora, Last.fm does not explain why it recommended any of its selections or how they are similar to "Thunder." It wouldn't be able to, as it lacks Pandora's depth of musical knowledge. When I try for matches with "Pashmina," Last.fm is unable to offer any recommendations. My guess is that reflects the fact that not many of Last.fm's users have listened to that track, and the site simply lacks the data on which to base "People who listened to 'Pashmina' also listened to . . ." recommendations.

What collaborative filters lack in depth of knowledge, though,

they make up for in simplicity. Because they don't require detailed information about product attributes, they are easy to
implement and roll out in a short period of time, and have therefore become the most popular class of automated product rec-
ommenders on the internet. And they work very well in practice.
If someone else likes something you like, you probably share
some underlying tastes or personality. Furthermore, merely knowing that someone like you favors something makes you *feel* that
you will like it as well. That feeling alone might be enough to
convince you that the recommendation is relevant.

These two design approaches can be used to recommend not
only music but also videos (Netflix, YouTube), news (Google
News), or, for that matter, any product on retail websites (Amazon). Unlike music and product recommendation algorithms,
algorithms at Facebook, LinkedIn, and Tinder recommend people. Which friend should you connect with on Facebook? Whom
should you date on Tinder? Linking people is arguably a harder
task, because the match has to be mutual. As Amarnath Thombre, CEO of Match.com and a director at Tinder, observes:
"Even if you like *The Godfather*, the Godfather doesn't have to
like you back." On Match.com, a match that is good for one
person but not the other has limited value.

I mull whether to extend my music experiment to Tinder,
and create a profile (with a "just for research" note appended).
My wife approves, to my slight surprise, but I worry that a student might discover the profile, not notice the disclaimer, and
start an interesting rumor or two about me. I get cold feet and

swipe left on the idea. Instead, I write to computer scientists who study "people recommendations" in social networks. They inform me that a common approach they take is to match based on similarities in demographic attributes—such as age, occupation, and location—or shared interests in topics and ideas discussed on social media. This feels a bit like Pandora's content-based approach: to match people, these algorithms attempt to accurately identify their interests, traits, and demographics. Of course, this can be limiting, because people with dissimilar interests can certainly have chemistry. But such matches are harder to establish, so recommendation algorithms take the easier route, and most people don't seem to mind. An alternative approach used by other algorithms relies on people's social networks themselves: for example, if you and I are not connected on LinkedIn but have more than a hundred mutual connections, we are notified that we should perhaps be connected. This approach makes no attempt to match people's interests or traits, but is more a collaborative "people connected to you are also connected to" method.

Both systems are intuitive, if not perfect, methods that we might use in our daily lives when we play matchmaker. They are both, in fact, based on *homophily*, a well-documented principle that describes our tendency to connect with those most like us.

In short, if you feel that recommendation algorithms are effective in helping you find relevant music, products, or people, it is because they are based on some fundamental principles of how we socialize in the real world. The real world, then, might be a good place for us to look next as we try to uncover how algorithms can lead us to listen to Khalid versus Coldplay, or read *If Nobody Speaks of Remarkable Things*.

———

Every Saturday morning I wake up early to join the tennis drills at Seger Park in Center City, Philadelphia. It's an essential part of my weekend routine as well as that of many others in the neighborhood. The drills are run by Joe Falzone, an unusual local business owner. His tennis store, located about a ten-minute walk from the park, looks like any other establishment of its kind. Joe is perhaps a bit more loquacious than average (advice: don't get him started about the time the US Open organizers sent him fifty tickets instead of the fifty-one that he had ordered), but that's not why I think he is an uncommon presence. Nor is it his backhand, which is also well above average. It's that he has been running his store for more than forty years—forty years during which Philadelphia's downtown has been through more than its share of ups and downs. And Joe's tennis store has lived through all these ebbs and flows and at least one missing ticket to the US Open.

Joe's business—and that of many of the nearby stores—has taken off in the last few years. There are more cafés in the neighborhood now, as well as more restaurants and shopping—and consequently, more foot traffic. Joe traces these changes to the construction of a new condominium nearby. "The neighborhood was labeled Philadelphia's 'gayborhood' and overlooked for so long. But who says they don't need cafés and restaurants?" he asks. Once the new building—and the associated commercial space that now houses many retail stores—appeared, people started moving into the area.

Location, location, location—it's talked about constantly in real estate. Being in the right neighborhood is one of the most important decisions a business can make, and Joe and his neighboring businesses had it made for them. But the principle extends far beyond just street locale. In grocery stores, similar items are placed next to one another on the same shelf; in bookstores, books of each genre are all shelved in the same section. These "neighborhoods" are valuable because they allow us to quickly find what we're looking for. So, whether you want to sell paintings, have people buy your jewelry, or advertise to a demographic making more than $100,000, you take the time to consider exactly what neighborhoods will best suit your needs.

In the physical world, this is not a new idea. But where do I go if I want to do these things online? Is there the equivalent of a neighborhood for a web-based business?

A friend once lamented, "If you have a 'real' store, you will have at least a few customers, just because they see your store as they walk or drive by the neighborhood. But on the internet, you can set up a store, and no one might find out about it." So is there no such thing as a digital neighborhood, an online analogue of Manhattan's Fifth Avenue?

One way to create *digital* neighborhoods is to organize webpages by category. During the early days of the World Wide Web, Yahoo and Geocities became successful web portals by translating the directory paradigm—classifying businesses by what products or services they offer—to the web and organizing websites into different categories. This enabled early internet users to browse the directory and find a satisfying selection of websites selling, say, collectible toys. But as the amount of information online grew, this means of organization started to reach its limit. As the neighborhood of websites offering toys grew from the size of Greenwich Village to the size of New York City, visitors found the neighborhood unnavigable. Today even the most niche topic has millions of webpages—"vintage model toy trains" returns more than seventy-six million results on Google.

Algorithms—whether in the form of search engines, recommendation systems, or social news feeds—emerged to help us manage the information explosion. However, what I have come to realize from running digital marketing campaigns with many startups is that while the approach to organizing the chaos online has changed, the significance of digital neighborhoods has not. They merely surface in different ways.

Google's founders, Larry Page and Sergey Brin, were able to successfully organize the world's information because they had the insight of viewing the web as neighborhoods of websites connected not just by topics and keywords, but by the web's native language of hyperlinks. In 1999, the most popular online search engines relied primarily on the text content within webpages to determine their relevance. Page and Brin realized that the key to understanding the web wasn't to focus on what was within a webpage, but to focus on what happens *between* them. Google's famous PageRank algorithm ranks webpages not only by the occurrence of search terms on those pages but also by the hyperlinks from other pages ("inlinks") that a page receives. The basic idea is to use the hyperlink as a signal of quality: if a lot of other websites have links to your website, then your site must be worth reading.* As in many spheres of life, it's not what you know but who you know that gets your website to rank higher.

Similarly, the value of Facebook's ad-targeting algorithms stems from its ability to understand neighborhoods of social connections: since similar people tend to be friends with one another, the company can infer an enormous amount of information about its users. This is why advertisers are willing to spend a lot of money on Facebook, targeting friends of their brand-loyal customers.

---

*Every algorithmic choice has consequences, sometimes unintended. In September 2006, a search for "miserable failure" on Google brought up the official biography of then U.S. President George W. Bush as the top search result, even though the phrase was not mentioned anywhere in the biography. Several online users had colluded and written blog posts with the text "miserable failure" and linked that text to George Bush's biography webpage. Because PageRank prioritized inlinks over the actual text, the page soon became the top result. This is a practice known as "Google bombing."

And at the heart of Amazon's shopping engine is its recommendation system, which has a detailed representation of product neighborhoods. Recommendations such as "people who viewed this product also viewed these other products" are links between products that create a "network" of interconnected goods.

It is these networks of interconnected websites, people, and products that create the new neighborhoods in a digital world. And just as there is immense value for physical retailers in being in the right neighborhood, online businesses can benefit from being strategically located in their digital neighborhoods.

A case in point is Jon McGregor, the novelist introduced at the opening of this chapter. Despite a lack of obvious links, a noteworthy event in the spring of 2004 was responsible for the sudden interest in the United States in McGregor's *If Nobody Speaks of Remarkable Things*: Oprah's Book Club pick—that and the digital neighborhoods created by modern algorithms.

During a span of fifteen years, between 1996 and 2010, Oprah chose seventy books for her book club, most of which became best sellers. When she selected Carson McCullers's 1940 classic *The Heart Is a Lonely Hunter* in April 2004, the result was no different. The book had been a hit in its time, but by the beginning of the twenty-first century it was getting its most significant sales boosts from English professors who had adopted it for their courses. After Oprah picked the novel, McGregor appeared to be pulled along with her. But why?

The Heart Is a Lonely Hunter and *If Nobody Speaks of Remarkable Things* share some thematic and stylistic similarities: both are set in anonymized towns where the authors had themselves lived, and both tell stories of individuals who might seem unremarkable at first glance. Both were published when the authors were in their twenties. But the detail that made the difference for McGregor's book in April 2004 had less to do with its quality or his biography than with its positioning. On the Amazon page for *The Heart Is a Lonely Hunter* was a list of books that "People who bought this book also bought." *If Nobody Speaks of Remarkable Things* was on this list.

The sales of McGregor's book dropped again a few months later, once the book was no longer being recommended on the pages of other popular titles. But was its temporary success just a coincidence? It's hard to conclusively prove that its sudden popularity was driven by its fortuitous placement in the digital neighborhood created by Amazon's algorithms. But there is a way to test that idea. Researchers at Tel Aviv University and New York University tracked the sales of all Oprah's book club picks as well as those of the books' "neighbors" in Amazon's recommendation network. They found that while Oprah's books benefited immensely, books recommended by Amazon next to her selections also experienced a significant increase in sales.

In recent research, my collaborator Anuj Kumar at the University of Florida and I further analyzed the economic significance of these digital neighborhoods. We found that for products that are more centrally located in the product network—i.e., those that are recommended on many other product pages—recommendation algorithms drive a dramatic increase in sales.

But products that are found at the edges of these digital neighborhoods—i.e., those that are not recommended on many other product pages—lose sales to the central products. Thus, it turns out that having the right location and neighbors in product networks is the digital equivalent of having a store on Fifth Avenue. And just as Joe Falzone's business took off due to choices made by real-estate developers, online sales of products can take off due to algorithm design choices made by software developers.

Amazon's decision to build a recommendation algorithm that employs collaborative filtering appears to have introduced a few more of us to McGregor's book than might otherwise have been the case. Wasn't this the promise of the internet—a democratization tool that would allow little-known book titles (or songs, or ideas) to finally get their due and blockbusters to cease to dominate our hearts, minds, and shopping carts?

It's an idea that was popularized in author Chris Anderson's book *The Long Tail*. He suggested that the main effect of automated recommendations would be to help people move from the world of hits to a world of niches—obscure products that are closer to our individual preferences but never get our attention in mainstream markets.

Like many others, I thought the idea made sense—up until the spring of 2006, when a PhD class I was teaching forced me to reconsider the notion entirely.

We were discussing the design of personalization algorithms used by Netflix, Amazon, and other online firms. Daniel Fleder, one of my students, asked if the design of common algorithms might not actually do the opposite—that is, reduce the diversity of items we consume. He suggested that collaborative filtering algorithms might be biased toward popular, rather than obscure, items because they recommend items based on what others are consuming.

Fleder's question intrigued me, and that summer we launched what became a series of studies on how algorithmic recommendations affect product discovery, and whether they aid or hurt niche products. In the first study I did with Fleder, we argued that because common recommendation algorithms promote products based on past sales and ratings ("people who bought X also bought Y"), they cannot recommend products that have only limited historical data, even if these products were likely to be rated favorably. That would skew the recommendations toward already popular products. We developed simulations of several commonly used recommendation algorithms to test the theory, and they indeed demonstrated that these algorithms can create a rich-get-richer effect for popular items.

To further test the theory, in a second study with Dokyun Lee at Carnegie Mellon University, we ran an experiment in partnership with a leading online retailer in Canada. A control group of about 500,000 users made purchase decisions without any exposure to algorithmic recommendations. A second group of 100,000 users was shown recommendations of the "people who bought X also bought Y" variety whenever they visited a product page.

We found, as expected, that recommendations increased purchases across multiple product categories, ranging from apparel and appliances to toys and video games. But purchase diversity is where the results got interesting. The figure below plots what economists refer to as a *Lorenz curve*, a graphical representation of how market share is distributed across all the products carried by the retailer. The X axis represents the products, from least sold on the left to most sold on the right. The Y axis is the proportion of total sales generated by these products. The black curved line is the Lorenz curve for the control group: the bot-

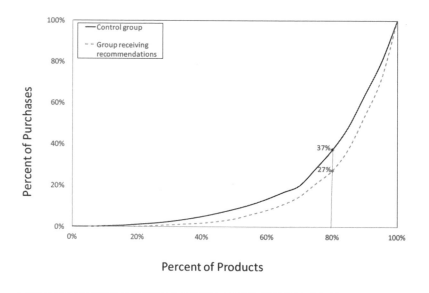

Market share distribution of products at a retailer

tom 40 percent of products generated roughly 5 percent of sales, and the bottom 80 percent about 37 percent of sales. The dotted curve shows the Lorenz curve for the users exposed to recommendations. The market share of niche products was even lower under recommendations. For example, the bottom 80 percent of products now generated only 27 percent of sales.

In addition to market share, we also looked at absolute sales of the products. Surprisingly, we found that the total sales of niche items went up. How is it possible that they were selling more at the same time that their market share was decreasing?

The answer to the puzzle lies in the fact that the sales for all items—niche as well as blockbuster—are greater under recommendations. Personalized recommendations help consumers discover many relevant items, and so they purchase far more than they did in the absence of recommendations. Although both niche and blockbuster items were purchased more, the gains were far greater for popular products than niche ones. As a result, niche sellers might notice that sales have risen, and individuals might notice they are consuming more esoteric items than before. But niche products are losing overall market share (and potentially consumer mindshare) under algorithmic recommendations.

It's a bit like what has happened to income levels in the United States over the last several decades. The average income, after taxes and government transfers, of the bottom 20 percent of earners has grown by 46 percent from 1979 to 2013, according to the Congressional Budget Office. But these gains are modest compared to the top 1 percent, which saw a 192 percent increase in income after taxes. While there are modest gains in absolute terms for the poor, the net result is growing income inequality.

We also found that although recommendation algorithms can push consumers to new products, they often push similar users toward the same products. So even though individuals might discover new items, aggregate diversity doesn't rise, and market share of popular items only increases.

Consider a well-known example documented in *The Long Tail*. Mountaineer Joe Simpson's *Touching the Void*, a book about an Andean climb gone awry, had nearly fallen out of print when *Into Thin Air*, Jon Krakauer's book about a disastrous day on Mount Everest, became a bestseller. Amazon's recommendation algorithms started suggesting *Touching the Void* to buyers of Krakauer's book, and the book experienced a sudden surge in sales. This case is often touted as an illustration of how an obscure title was discovered due to algorithmic recommendations, but I often wonder whether it actually serves as an example of the sales concentration that commonly used recommendation algorithms can create. On their own, all the readers of *Into Thin Air* might have bought a range of other books during subsequent purchases. Some shoppers might have found, say, Reinhold Messner's *The Naked Mountain*, an account of his famed climb of Nanga Parbat in the Himalayas. Others might have discovered Diane Sanfilippo's *Practical Paleo*, about the Paleo diet. And still others might have bought Salim Ali's *The Book of Indian Birds*. But if all of them were recommended *Touching the Void*, and many of them bought that title, aggregate diversity would decline. While each of these shoppers might experience being exposed to an obscure and very relevant title that they might have otherwise missed, in aggregate, diversity will be lower.

Why does this matter? The collaborative filter's bias toward popularity can stand in the way of better consumer-product matches that would have occurred if the algorithm paid attention to product attributes instead, à la Pandora. After all, wasn't the promise of recommendation algorithms to help us find the ideal music, movies, and products that the mainstream, blockbuster culture hides from us? Subsequent research by my group as well as a group at MIT found that content-based recommender designs are quite successful at surfacing those gems, independent of their popularity.

So, how do we get the best of both worlds—the simplicity and social appeal of a collaborative filter, and the knowledge and fairness of content-based designs?

This is, in fact, the question that motivates the third approach to recommendations. When music service Spotify rolled out its personalized music recommendations feature, the original algorithm was a collaborative filter. Recognizing the popularity bias of collaborative filters, Spotify's engineers subsequently created a hybrid design that combined the collaborative filter with a content-based method.

But wasn't the challenge of Pandora's approach allocating the time and effort involved in having musicologists listen to and collect musical attributes for each and every track? What if there was a way, however, to automate the work of musicologists at Pandora? In fact, Spotify crawls the web to examine blog posts and other online discussions about music to figure out the kind of descriptive language that listeners use to discuss different songs and artists. It then uses these terms for attributes of songs. But this step alone is insufficient, as new or niche songs aren't discussed as often online, so there is insufficient data about them. Spotify therefore additionally uses machine learning algorithms to analyze the audio signal of a song and extract its characteristics, such as tempo, loudness, key, and tonality. At the end of this process, its algorithms have a collaborative filter's understanding of music listening patterns as well as Pandora's deep understanding of the music itself.

The end result is Spotify's Discover Weekly, an algorithmically generated personalized weekly playlist. Spotify says that as many as 8,000 artists get more than half their streams from users listening to their Discover Weekly playlists. So, it appears that the approach is able to break free from the collaborative filter's popularity bias. And music fans seem to love it as well. One online user even tweeted: "My significant other better know me as well as my Discover Weekly."

———

Computer scientists, academics, and businesspeople have all tended to evaluate algorithms narrowly, focusing on a single performance metric that captures precisely what the programmer is trying to improve—for example, the accuracy of product recommendations. But we generally don't evaluate, let alone measure, algorithms holistically, considering all the ways in which they change their users' decisions—individually or in aggregate. And what doesn't get measured doesn't get caught. I didn't appreciate this point before conducting my 2006 study with Fleder. Since then, I always try to take into account the unintended consequences. I've noticed that other scientists are starting to take note, as well. Recent work on recommendation systems has looked beyond the accuracy of recommendations themselves (i.e., how often recommended items are relevant to the user) to consider the diversity of recommendations. Although the design of recommendation engines has been changing, we are still in the minority. Most other algorithms continue to be evaluated narrowly using one or two technical criteria and without regard to the kinds of metrics that keep social scientists awake at night—issues such as fairness, accountability, safety, and privacy.

Unintended consequences can arise even when every step of an algorithm is carefully designed by a programmer. The failure of the internet to uncover hidden gems is one simple example. But what happens when we move from product recommendation algorithms to more complex ones that can diagnose diseases or drive cars? Enter the world of AI and machine learning: a world where algorithms don't just make recommendations and suggestions, but make decisions completely autonomously. A world in which algorithms can go awry in far more dangerous ways.

4.

Algorithms Become Intelligent

A BRIEF HISTORY OF AI

Machines will be capable, within twenty years, of doing any work a man can do.

Herbert Simon, Nobel Laureate and Turing Prize winner, 1965

On May 28, 1783, Hungarian inventor Wolfgang von Kempelen wrote a letter to Benjamin Franklin, inviting him to the Paris hotel where Kempelen was staying to view "a very interesting machine" that had "mystified all the members of the Académie des sciences." Franklin, serving at the time as U.S. Ambassador to France, accepted the invitation and soon declared Kempelen a genius. The machine, called the Mechanical Turk, was an automated chess-playing robot bedecked in fur-lined robes and a turban. It was shown throughout Europe for the next eight decades, playing against such eminences as Napoleon Bonaparte, Edgar Allan Poe, and Franklin himself. Usually, it won—though it was defeated by François-André Danican Philidor, the European chess champion of the era who nonetheless admitted it was the most tiring game he had ever played. A young Charles Babbage, whom many credit with creating the first conceptual design for a programmable computer, was so enthralled that, years later, he harked back to the Mechanical Turk in arguing that chess was among the most compelling applications for his Analytical Engine.

By then, Kempelen's machine had a number of detractors, and indeed, it turned out that the device had never been an automaton at all, but rather "an elaborate hoax involving a hidden human player, an articulated mechanical arm, and a series of magnetic linkages." Still, scientists and engineers had believed in it, perhaps because the dream of artificial intelligence is itself so enchanting.

It took another 150 years or so before that fantasy began to be approached with the tools of science rather than of trickery.

In 1950, the true scientific foundations for AI were laid when the English mathematician Alan Turing published a paper posing a simple question: "Can machines think?" Turing imagined a scenario in which a computer might chat with humans and trick them into believing that it, too, was human. This hypothesized imitation game became known as the Turing test, and established an ambitious milestone by which to measure the intelligence of machines thereafter.

Soon after, the American computer scientist John McCarthy

proposed a workshop that would engage with just this quest, seeking to discover how to make machines solve the kinds of problems that only humans were assumed to be capable of solving. And yet McCarthy struggled to raise funds. Turing's question may have been provocative, but how one might actually address it was a prospect that many people could not get their heads around. A representative from The Rockefeller Foundation, to which McCarthy appealed for money, observed, "The general feeling here is that this new field of mathematical models for thought . . . is still difficult to grasp very clearly." Nevertheless, the foundation reluctantly gave him $7,500 to organize the event.

At the time, researchers in this area had been focusing on narrow fields with names such as automata studies, cybernetics, and information processing. In McCarthy's view, none of these research areas encompassed the significance of the revolution ahead, and none had a name that would help outsiders understand the enormity of what was being studied. In one attempt to address this, he urged the mathematician Claude Shannon to change the title of a book he'd written, which was to be called *Automata Studies*. McCarthy deemed this too conservative; Shannon rejected the suggestion. But McCarthy got his chance when naming his conference, which he called the Dartmouth Summer Research Project on Artificial Intelligence, thus, historians believe, coining the term. "Calling it AI made it extremely ambitious, and it inspired many people to enter the field, which has been responsible for a lot of the progress. At the same time, it also created these highly inflated expectations," Pedro Domingos, a computer scientist at the University of Washington, Seattle, noted during our recent conversation.

The workshop eventually took place in the summer of 1956 and drew about twenty experts. From it emerged the scaffolding on which AI today is built: the recognition that human-level intelligence is the gold standard to aim for in machines. "I think the main thing [the workshop established] was the concept of artificial intelligence as a branch of science. Just this inspired many people to pursue AI goals in their own ways," McCarthy later remarked. The conference confirmed that Turing's questions, however enormous, were the ones that best framed this new field: What is thinking, what are machines, where do the two meet, how, and to what end?

By then Alan Turing had died tragically at the age of forty-two, of cyanide poisoning—whether as the result of an accident or suicide remains unclear. He never attended any large gathering of AI scientists. However, the workshop was attended by another pioneer, Herb Simon, who in 1978 would receive the Nobel Prize in Economics. His most important contribution to economics was pointing out the deficiency in the dominant economic model of decision making at the time—and still a commonly used model in microeconomics—which held that people make perfectly rational decisions to maximize their utility. Instead he suggested that, because of practical constraints such as limited time and the cognitive burden of decision making, people often seek a satisfactory solution rather than the perfectly optimal one. Simon's notion of *bounded rationality* was a cornerstone for the field of behavioral economics. He also won the Turing Award, which is often described as the Nobel of computer science, for his contributions to the founding of AI.*

A few months prior to attending the Dartmouth workshop, Simon told one of his classes that "over the Christmas holiday, Al Newell and I invented a thinking machine." Simon and Newell had built the first symbolic software program, which they called the Logic Theorist. The software proved the theorems presented in the seminal three-volume *Principia Mathematica*, by Bertrand Russell and Alfred North Whitehead, and even "[proved] one theorem more elegantly than had Russell and Whitehead," according to one historian of science. In response to this tremendous feat of engineering, Russell himself observed, "I [only] wish Whitehead and I had known of this possibility before we both wasted ten years doing it by hand."

By 1959 Newell and Simon had built the first general problem solver that could tackle a broad class of problems expressed

---

*In January 2000, as a first-year PhD student at Carnegie Mellon University, I had the chance to meet with and learn from Herb Simon when I enrolled in his class on Cognitive Psychology. Despite Simon's exceptional credentials, I was somewhat bored in the classroom. In a conversation with my friend Josh back in 2000, I once remarked "Well, he may be an amazing researcher but he is not a great teacher." To this day, Josh ribs me, asking "He *may* be an amazing researcher? So you aren't sure?" Boy, don't you hate those friends who remember every stupid thing you ever said?

as well-formed formulae. For many observers, this software pro-gram demonstrated that artificial intelligence could be created by humans, cementing Simon and colleagues' place as pioneers in the AI revolution.*

By the mid-1960s, the AI community's ambitions had grown. "Machines will be capable, within twenty years, of doing any work a man can do," Simon declared. By 1967 Mac Hack VI, developed by engineers at MIT, became the first computer to enter a human chess tournament and win a game. At the time, the AI community used a number of different approaches to build intelligent systems. Some, such as Simon, relied on rules of logic. Others used statistical techniques to infer probabilities of events based on data. (For a familiar contemporary example, if an email contains words such as "free money" and "get out of debt," then the probability that the email is spam rises.) And still others used neural networks, a technique inspired by how a net-

---

*I did once ask Herb Simon's advice on a research project of mine. I wanted to build a search engine that retrieves information from the web in the same way that a human brain retrieves information from memory. I visited him in his office and asked some questions about how the human brain works. My ideas were half-baked at best, and yet he was incredibly kind and generous, explaining short- and long-term memory retrieval processes, and how they differ. He never discouraged me in the least, but I realized from this conversation that this search engine I envisaged was a tall order. I decided to move on to another problem: how to build a comparison-shopping search engine that could list the set of online stores that carry a product as well as the product price at each of the stores. That ended up becoming the very first research paper of my PhD. The challenge was relatively simple, tractable, and practical, but not the kind of grand problem that Simon had spent a lifetime tack-ling. So I didn't go back to share my paper with him when it was published. I some-times regret that.

work of neurons in the human brain fires to create new knowledge or validate existing knowledge. However, this approach lost favor in the community in 1969 when Marvin Minsky, an AI pioneer and one of the attendees of the original Dartmouth conference, along with his colleague Seymour Papert, published a book, *Perceptrons*, outlining the limitations of neural networks. Their criticisms soon became commonly held beliefs, and most people in the research community dropped neural networks in favor of other approaches. In hindsight, the understanding of how best to build neural networks was limited, and the computing resources that were available back then were insufficient for such sophisticated techniques. "Your brain is the best supercomputer on earth, and people were trying to do this through the computer that they had back then. They ran a little bit ahead of themselves," says Domingos.

During the following decade considerable funding went into the field, but like the 1970s itself, this was a period of over-promising and under-delivering. By the 1980s financial backers from both government and industry grew frustrated at not seeing grand applications of AI come to fruition. So an "AI winter" set in. Funding for AI plummeted and was directed instead to other areas of computer science, such as networking, databases, and information retrieval. Media coverage of AI decreased as well. Creating machine intelligence was, it turned out, a harder problem than its advocates anticipated. Humans sometimes take their own intelligence for granted, forgetting that evolution spent hundreds of millions of years refining it—and that process is far from complete. The field had to set more-realistic near-term goals.

The AI winter resulted in a shift in the kinds of problems researchers and engineers tackled. Previously their target had been *artificial general intelligence* (AGI)—AI with human-level intelligence that could be applied to all kinds of tasks, also described as "strong AI." This was now considered to be not just too ambitious, but the wrong path. The focus turned to more practical systems, with an emphasis on methods that were more likely to deliver.

The most prominent of these was the *expert systems* approach: manually programming software with specific knowledge and sets of rules. Imagine interviewing a doctor and codifying the diagnostic rules he follows to automate the process. Expert systems, in fact, were the main driver of an AI spring in the 1990s. Strong early results led to renewed funding and reengaged the public interest, particularly when on May 11, 1997, IBM's Deep Blue computer defeated Garry Kasparov, then the world's highest-rated chess player in recorded history, winning the six-game series 3.5–2.5. Nathan Ensmenger, a historian of computing, refers to its victory as "one of the pivotal moments in the history of modern computing."

And yet there were limits to the capabilities of expert systems. For one thing, they tended to excel at narrow, specialized tasks, and as such were known as *artificial narrow intelligence* (ANI), or "weak AI." For another, whenever expert systems algorithms encountered a situation that they were not explicitly programmed to handle, they failed. "In the end, [expert systems] mostly failed because the systems were too brittle," explains Domingos.

By the early 2000s, researchers were starting to recognize that computers could never attain true intelligence without machine learning. The emphasis switched back to algorithms that could adapt—that could recognize completely new situations and reason their way through them. Such algorithms may function poorly when they are first developed, since they lack some of the detailed instructions that expert systems might contain. But they learn from data and get better over time.

—————

The advent of the internet meant relatively easy access to large datasets that could be used to train machine learning algorithms. This Big Data revolution was accompanied by the greater availability of specialized processors that had originally been designed to handle 3-D graphics in gaming but that could also be used to process large datasets. Two critical ingredients were now in place for a successful return of machine learning. And an additional key ingredient was fast emerging: a paradigm shift in how to approach the problem.

As a PhD student, I studied simple statistical machine learning methods to handle tasks such as detecting spam. The tools created using these methods would take in large training datasets of emails with clear labels for spam as well as legitimate messages, and could automatically learn the kinds of words, phrases, and linguistic patterns associated with spam. These tools worked very well. In one study conducted in 2013, my research group sought to determine what characteristics—emotion, humor, brand mentions, philanthropic messaging, et cetera— were present in the social media content posted by companies on Facebook. We first created a training dataset of 5,000 messages in which characteristics such as emotion and humor were labeled by humans. Machine learning algorithms were trained on this data and then used to automatically identify content characteristics for more than 100,000 other messages. Over several months, we evaluated and fine-tuned multiple machine learning methods and eventually arrived at one that could identify content characteristics with more than 95 percent accuracy. (Accuracy is the percentage of predictions that are correct: if a spam filter evaluates 100 emails, predicts whether they are spam or not, and gets 97 predictions right, then its accuracy is 97 percent.)

But we—and others—also found that these approaches had their limits. In traditional machine learning methods, a programmer usually specifies what patterns to look for. For example, a spam-detection algorithm might be asked to look at individual words, two-word phrases, three-word phrases, parts of speech, and other specific linguistic patterns. The algorithm examines these patterns in a training dataset and determines which ones are most closely associated with spam. While the performance (measured, for example, by accuracy) of these traditional machine learning methods improves as they are exposed to greater amounts of data, this holds true only up to a limit. At some point, performance stops improving, no matter how much additional data is fed. This was one reason why these methods were not overwhelmingly successful at complex perceptual tasks such as recognizing and synthesizing speech (think Siri) or recognizing and tracking vehicles on a road (think autonomous vehicles).

The more immediate reason behind the recent explosion in machine learning is the advances in *deep learning*, a term for digital neural networks arranged in several layers. In deep learning, programmers don't specify what patterns to look for: the algorithm evaluates the training data in different ways to identify the patterns that truly matter—patterns that human programmers might not even notice. Deep learning models contain an input layer that represents the input data, an output layer with the desired prediction, and multiple hidden layers in between that combine patterns from previous layers to identify abstract and complex patterns in the data. For example, the input layer for a face recognition deep learning model might simply record the RGB (red, green, blue) values of all the pixels of an input image. Its intermediate, hidden layers might combine these simple values to identify patterns such as eye shape or the size of foreheads. The patterns identified in the hidden layers might ultimately lead the model to the output—say, the name of the person in the image.

While neural networks may have gone out of fashion after Minsky's criticism of the method, they didn't completely disappear. In the 1980s Geoff Hinton, then a professor at Carnegie

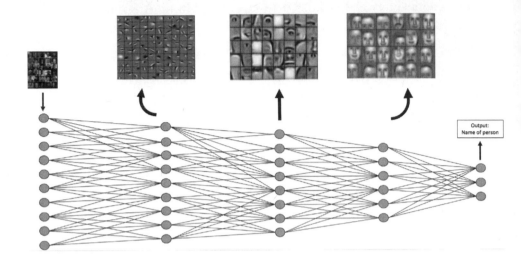

Hidden layers in deep learning models identify patterns such as eye shape or the size of foreheads (based on an original image by Andrew Ng)

Mellon, currently at both Google and the University of Toronto, along with his colleagues developed a fast algorithm for training neural networks with multiple layers. Over the next several years, many other researchers built on this foundational work. All their efforts came to fruition in 2012 when Hinton's research group won (by a significant margin) the ImageNet Challenge, a contest in which teams compete to build the best image recognition algorithms.

That deep learning approaches have done better at exploiting the modern explosion in data is nicely illustrated in a graph (see figure on next page) by Andrew Ng, a Stanford computer science professor and former Chief Scientist at Baidu. This figure shows how the performance of older algorithms plateaus much earlier than that of modern deep learning algorithms. The strength of deep learning algorithms is not that they can merely accommodate the explosion in data, but that they actually thrive on it. It is hard to overstate the value of data in modern machine learning. More data means more examples for algorithms to learn from, and more examples lead to an unprecedented increase in accuracy.

The combination of massive datasets, processing power, and deep learning methods has brought machine learning back to center stage and is enabling all kinds of modern miracles, from algorithms that can extract musical attributes of a song from its audio signal (à la Spotify) to ones that can diagnose diseases.

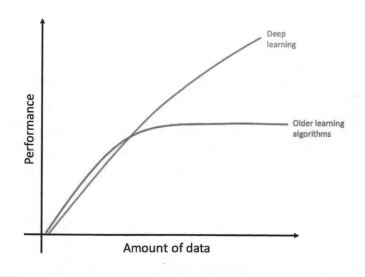

Performance of machine learning methods versus quantum of training data (based on an original graph by Andrew Ng)

In 1970 Jack Myers, a respected internist and head of the University of Pittsburgh's Department of Medicine, began recording his thoughts during the process of diagnosing patients. He was not writing a book or preparing a course, but working alongside computer scientists to create a machine that could itself accurately diagnose patients' ailments. Myers's role was to teach the machine everything he knew. Given these relatively primitive data collection methods, the result was astounding—a machine that could "match 3,550 symptoms with more than 500 diseases that made up about three-quarters of the diagnoses in internal medicine," according to *The New York Times*.

The system, called Internist-1/Caduceus, eventually expanded its abilities, in part by taking in greater volumes of expert instruction via coded medical research papers. Still, while it was celebrated for its success in augmenting a human doctor's experience and skills, it earned poor marks as a stand-in physician. (It earned a C-minus grade alongside similar systems from a mid-1990s reviewer in the *New England Journal of Medicine*.)

For all the time and energy that Myers devoted to the machine, his experience demonstrates that as we move from relatively simple tasks, such as providing product recommendations, to more challenging ones, such as diagnosing diseases, we are also moving closer in scope and challenge to the "Can machines think?" question that Turing originally posed.

Expert systems such as Internist-1 suffered from two major

deficiencies that disqualified them from being called truly intelligent. First, they were not automating the full process of diagnosis. Luke Oakden-Rayner, an Australian radiologist, computer science researcher, and blogger who has written extensively on this subject, argues that the truly time-consuming portion of being a diagnostician is not processing all the information to arrive at a final opinion. He argues that experienced doctors arrive at a diagnosis within seconds through a simple process of pattern recognition. Doctors spend most of their time exercising their five senses—listening to a patient's chest, noting his pallor—to help capture the relevant information. "For decades, machines were no good at this sort of 'human-like' perception," Oakden-Rayner writes. Expert systems like Internist "asked a doctor to do all the perception and then automated the decision making. It was a problem that was solvable, but it wasn't . . . valuable." Deep learning algorithms, however, *are* good at perception—already as good as humans at a variety of tasks. (One obvious example is your smartphone's voice transcriber.)

A second drawback to expert systems is that manually coding how a software program should respond to every kind of situation it might encounter can seem like an endless task for a programmer, especially as systems become increasingly complex. Consider the task of programming a driverless car's motion-planning system—in other words, its driving policy, essentially the strategy it uses to negotiate traffic and other on-road situations such as lane closures and accidents. An expert-system approach to the problem involves identifying and programming a set of rules that all of us instinctively follow when we drive: rules such as "Do not hit a pedestrian" and "Do not run into trees," as well as rules we should follow but which many people don't, such as "Use an indicator before changing lanes."

A startup called nuTonomy recently launched a fleet of driverless taxis in Singapore using an approach along these lines. The company's driving policy consists entirely of a hierarchy of rules; some, such as "Do not hit a pedestrian," may have higher priority than others, such as "Stop for a yellow light." Based on data about its current driving environment, the vehicle evaluates in real time the potential paths it can take and selects one that best complies with the rule hierarchy.

Google's self-driving car prototypes, in contrast, aren't based on rules programmed by human experts. Instead, the Google algorithm was trained on a database of videos of humans driving, and developed its own driving policy using machine learning. Next, like a fifteen-year-old learning to drive alongside a parent, it racked up miles driving cars on public roads with a safety driver observing its decisions. The difference lies in the numbers: the algorithm drove a few million miles during its training stage, something not even the most enthusiastic teen motorhead could manage. Today, the car drives on its own, having taught itself how to best react to road conditions.

Google is hardly the only entity switching from expert systems approaches to machine learning. In 2015 researchers at the Mount Sinai hospital system in New York used an alternative approach to Myers's in building an automated medical diagnostic tool. Rather than interview medical experts and build a system of diagnostic rules from their input, they fed data from 700,000 patients to a deep learning algorithm. The algorithm analyzed these patients' medical test reports and the diagnoses human doctors had reached, and inferred which medical markers predicted which medical conditions.

The system, DeepPatient, detected patterns and taught itself to diagnose without being programmed with a single diagnostic rule. It worked incredibly well, not just with simple diagnoses, such as strep throat, but with extremely complicated ones, such as the onset of schizophrenia, which are difficult for even experienced doctors to diagnose. And it doesn't make patients wait for an hour in a waiting room.

———

These examples might make the expert systems versus machine learning approaches seem black-and-white: ineffective versus highly functional systems. In fact, both are legitimate ways to build artificial intelligence, but they entail very different trade-offs for society. What are these trade-offs? And which approach is likely to dominate in the future? For the answers, we return first to our old friend, the chess-playing Mechanical Turk. Or rather, to his present-day avatar: the game-playing automaton.

5.

Machine Learning and the Predictability-Resilience Paradox

> The mind is a complex and many-layered thing, Potter . . . or at least, most minds are.
>
> J. K. Rowling, *Harry Potter and the Order of the Phoenix*

> Almost everything we do in the technological realm seems to lead us away from elegance and understandability, and toward impenetrable complexity and unexpectedness.
>
> Samuel Arbesman, *Overcomplicated*

One day in the autumn of 2003, my former PhD student Dokyun Lee, then a student at Stuyvesant High School in New York City, sat in front of a chessboard at his after-school chess club. He found himself, however, preoccupied with memories of a lesser-known and older (by about a thousand years) strategy game he had played as a kid in Korea: Go. He had rapidly risen up its skill levels to the rank of 1-Dan, an advanced amateur status a few steps away from professional. (1-Dan is equivalent to martial arts' black belt.)

Dokyun decided to start a Go club at his school so that his friends could experience the game as well. To rope in other students, he described Go as a game that is "so easy to learn but needs a lifetime to master." The tagline intrigued a few of his classmates that first year, and over time the Go club grew to be as large as the chess club.

Chess and Go are similar in some ways: both are two-player face-offs where one player controls white game pieces and the other black. In each, the players take turns, making one move per turn; pieces are captured, and the driving metaphors are those of battle and war. Both originated in Asia—chess in India and Go in China.

But where the goal of chess is to capture the king, Go is won by taking and securing territory; also, in chess the pieces have different powers and can move around the board, while in Go they do not and cannot. At first glance, Go might seem simpler, but it is, in fact, more complex. Mathematicians estimate that there are more possible valid positions in Go than atoms in the universe, and it is this feature that has been of particular interest to the world of AI.

From the Mechanical Turk to IBM's Deep Blue, "intelligent" machines have been measured by their skill at the game of kings. But even Deep Blue's programmers approached the challenge of winning at chess in a way that would leave the machine poorly positioned to beat a human at a round of Go. They had coded the rules of chess into Deep Blue's software, and even though its knowledge of the game came from its human programmers, the machine's victory over Kasparov was the result of brute computation—the ability to explore 200 million possible chess positions in a second before choosing a move with the greatest likelihood of success. It was, in other words, an expert system with the trump card of superhuman processing power.

Go's complexity makes it impossible to win via pure computational strength. This means that creativity—the province of sentient beings—is required to prevail. Lee Sedol, the Go world champion from Korea, believes that Go "is the only game that truly balances the left and right sides of the brain." This explains why Go-playing software had struggled against human grandmasters despite Deep Blue's success at chess. That changed in March 2016 when Lee Sedol fell in a five-game tournament to Google's Go-playing computer program, AlphaGo.

Dokyun, who graduated from Stuyvesant and went on to study AI (eventually becoming a data scientist and an important influence on my own work), had been told in all his undergraduate and grad school classes that we were still a few decades away from developing an AI system that could crack Go. His teachers were wrong.

How did Google's software achieve this feat? And why does AlphaGo's victory matter to anyone other than game enthusiasts like Dokyun?

AlphaGo wasn't based on rules programmed by human experts; instead, it programmed its own rules using machine learning. It was trained on a database of more than 30 million past moves by expert Go players. Additionally, it played millions of games against itself—more than "the number of games played by the entire human race since the creation of Go," according to the research team that created it. This preparation came to fruition most vividly in the second game of the Sedol-AlphaGo match of March 2016. After a resounding defeat in game 1, Sedol was playing more carefully, and even though AlphaGo had gained a slight early edge, the contest was still anyone's to win. Then move 37 happened.

AlphaGo, playing black, made an unusual move on the center-right side of the board. "I thought it was a mistake," said one commentator within seconds of the play. Sedol stepped out of the room briefly and took nearly fifteen minutes to respond. Fan Hui, a European Go champion who had previously lost to AlphaGo, remarked "It's not a human move. I've never seen a human play this move." He later described it as "so beautiful. So beautiful." AlphaGo went on to win the game (and I hope was a good sport about it).

Move 37 was, in fact, in some ways an utterly human move— the kind of mysterious, creative, and unpredictable action of which humans are routinely capable but that we don't expect from machines. What made it unusual was that it couldn't be understood by AlphaGo's human developers, let alone programmed by them. They had simply provided the input—millions of Go moves from past games—and stood back to observe the output: that stunning 37th move.

Given that such deep learning systems independently combine simple concepts to create abstract patterns from the data, computer scientists don't actually know what's going on under the hood of their systems. How or why AlphaGo and its peers behave in certain ways is often not clear even to their designers.

Why might this be disturbing? On the one hand, there is the sheer eeriness of computers displaying the sort of creativity that we believed belonged to humans alone. But there is also a more practical concern. Think about the way we teach young children to operate in the world. We might simply give them sets of rules and watch, satisfied, as they follow them: wash your hands before eating; wait your turn; wrestle that winter coat on by laying it on the floor, sticking your hands in the arm openings, and flipping it over your head. But children also routinely surprise us, pretending to have washed their hands when they've patently not done so; finding another activity rather than waiting in line to do the original one; deciding that they're coordinated enough to put on a jacket the way they've seen adults do it, one arm at a time. Such abilities are not the result of following sets of rules they have been taught but rather stem from observing people around them and picking up new skills on their own. A capacity to surprise is core to a child's normal development. It also makes them admittedly difficult to handle at times.

The same is true of algorithms. Today, some of the most accurate machine learning models that computer scientists can build are also the most opaque. As machines become more intelligent and dynamic they also become more unpredictable. This suggests a fundamental conundrum in algorithm design. You can either create intelligent algorithms in highly curated environments—for example, programming explicit rules they might follow, expert systems style—to ensure they are highly predictable in behavior, while accepting that they will run up against problems they weren't prepared for and therefore can't solve; or, you can expose them to messy real-world data to create resilient but also unpredictable algorithms. I call this a *predictability-resilience paradox.*

The unpredictability of a game-playing algorithm may not be particularly troublesome to anyone outside the Go universe. However, when life-altering decisions are placed in the cybernetic hands of algorithms, the ability to understand and predict their decisions becomes more urgent. We can't always know why an airline pilot pulled rather than pushed the control wheel amid turbulence; why a manager decided to hire someone with nontraditional qualifications; why a doctor decided not to order a blood test for her patient. And yet most of us find unfathomable the idea that we would let computers make these decisions and *still* not know the reasoning. But as much as we may desire fully explainable and interpretable algorithms, the balance between predictability and resilience inevitably seems to be tilting in the latter direction.

———

At the heart of predictable systems is a set of rules—essentially a series of "if-then" statements that enable designers to know how the algorithm will behave under a certain set of conditions. This is both the strength and inherent weakness of these algorithms. In many situations, their predictability is a good thing. Consider, for example, tax software that is designed to help you take advantage of all available deductions and write-offs. While the United States tax code is extremely complicated, it is also entirely deterministic. Whether you can or cannot write off a particular expense depends on a long but finite set of parameters: your annual gross income, your marital status, the number of dependents you can claim, whether you run your own business, et cetera. The designers of tax software know this, and use a series of simple questions and an elaborate series of if-then rules to guide you through the process of filing your taxes. In contexts where the answer depends on a deterministic set of rules, predictable systems clearly provide the best possible performance.

However, there are many reasons why we may want to move beyond purely predictable systems. For one, the vast range of human experience and decision making cannot be governed by a simple set of articulable rules. What are the rules for writing a blockbuster movie script, or for negotiating a contract? What are the rules for deciding whether someone deserves parole or not? Indeed, research from many disciplines has demonstrated that the majority of humans make most of their decisions on the basis of inarticulable knowledge—in other words, instinct.

This phenomenon is crystallized in what MIT economist David Autor refers to as *Polanyi's paradox*: "We know more than we can tell." In his 1966 book, *The Tacit Dimension*, the Anglo-Hungarian mathematician-turned-philosopher Michael Polanyi made the argument that much of scientific inquiry is driven by tacit knowledge and an innate sense of knowing. Not only is this an interesting philosophical premise, but it has an enormous impact on the practical concerns around the design of algorithms.

The truth of Polanyi's paradox can be easily grasped when you are forced to codify some of the knowledge you take for granted every day. Imagine you had to describe what your mother's face looked like in a way that would enable someone else to pick her out of a crowd. While you could, of course, find your own mother among a group of thousands of people, someone using your written description would likely struggle to identify her even among only a few dozen. Ultimately, Polanyi's paradox argues that decision systems that are codified and articulable must by their very nature be limited. They are usually brittle systems—easily breakable, that is to say. When they are confronted with examples or challenges that their instructions aren't designed to handle, predictable systems fail miserably.

Yet another shortcoming of predictable systems is that they

can be easily manipulated. Just as there will always be con men trying to exploit the weaknesses of their fellow humans, algorithmic systems are constantly subjected to deliberate manipulation and deception.

At the heart of Google's $700 billion empire is its search engine, and at the heart of its search engine is its ranking algorithm. Back in 1999 Google cofounders Larry Page and Sergey Brin published a detailed description of their PageRank algorithm online. While it has some mathematical subtleties, PageRank is ultimately a fairly predictable algorithm: the more times your website is linked to from other websites, the higher it will be ranked in search results. However, because Google's algorithm was both public and predictable, it created a perverse incentive for many website owners to generate "shadow" websites whose sole purpose was to link back to their primary domain.

As such, much of the engineering effort at Google in recent years has been devoted not only to improving the results of the web-ranking algorithms, but also to fighting spam and the work of search engine manipulators. After its initial stint of intellectual openness, Google has grown famously secretive about which factors affect a website's position in its search results. More recently, its ranking algorithm has leaned heavily on machine learning principles, based on data about which results got the most engagement from previous searchers.

Google is only one of the many companies that have seen their predictable algorithms manipulated and reverse-engineered. Instagram and Twitter are battling armies of bot and spam accounts whose sole purpose is to like and repost other accounts, boosting the spammers' position in the platforms' ranking algorithms. And manipulability will only become an increasing concern as algorithms come to be used in other domains with more serious consequences. Suppose a fraudster knew exactly what rules credit card companies used to flag suspicious activity, or a terrorist knew exactly what TSA screening systems were looking for in their image-processing algorithms. With that knowledge, it would become easy to avoid detection.

To be clear, machine learning systems can also be manipulated. Researchers at the University of Washington found that even simple changes to street signs—for example, putting stickers on stop signs—could confuse the image recognition software in self-driving cars. They pointed out that vandalism in the form of stickers and graffiti on road signs could cause these systems to behave in "unexpected and potentially dangerous ways." Just as programmers might neglect to teach self-driving vehicles about altered road signs, the (albeit vast) datasets on which machine learning trains might also lack such images, leaving the cars flummoxed when they encounter them. As a result of these considerations, interest is growing in the area of *adversarial machine learning*, which involves learning from data that may be intentionally manipulated by adversaries trying to trip the system.

That said, the experience of Google and other tech companies indicates that predictable algorithms remain the easiest to reverse-engineer and game for nefarious purposes. But because Polanyi's paradox suggests that our ability to codify our most interesting and important abilities is severely limited, if we limit algorithms only to solving problems that are easily codified, we will relegate technology to such stodgy domains as tax codes. Technology is most useful when it helps us solve the most creative problems we face as human beings. And using technology to solve these problems effectively will require us to move away from predictable systems.

What does it take to discover treatments for rare diseases? Deep knowledge of medicine? Access to biochemistry labs? Familiarity with biotechnology and pharmacology? If your answer to all of these questions is yes, then perhaps you haven't heard the story of the late Don Swanson, who was an information scientist at the University of Illinois at Chicago.

Swanson was an avid runner who completed a half marathon at the age of eighty. But in his younger years, he suffered from Raynaud's syndrome, a condition that causes blood vessels to constrict in response to low temperatures or stress. It is not the sort of condition that kills people, but it can affect their quality of life. In its common form, symptoms include a numb, prickly feeling or stinging pain in the fingers and toes. In severe cases, limited blood circulation can cause tissue damage and warrant amputation.

While investigating another matter entirely, Swanson began reading about the Inuit diet, and one detail of it—high fish consumption—caught his attention. The research suggested that elevated fish oil intake increases blood flow, reduces blood vessels' reactions to cold, and inhibits platelet-triggered clotting. These changes in the blood system, Swanson happened to know, were all associated with Raynaud's. Fish oil, he hypothesized, might help treat the syndrome.

When a medical researcher comes up with such a hypothesis, he or she heads to the lab to test it. But what does an information scientist do? Swanson headed to the library. He found many studies that confirmed that fish oil improved blood circulation, but none of the existing research even suggested that it was an effective treatment for Raynaud's. In 1986 Swanson wrote a research paper proposing the idea. In 1989 a clinical study conducted on Raynaud's patients at the rheumatology clinic at Albany Medical College confirmed his hypothesis.

Swanson's work marked an important moment in science. The treatment for Raynaud's disease wasn't discovered by medical researchers with deep knowledge of rheumatology or the chemical makeup of fish oil, but by an information scientist armed with data on thousands of prior studies and the insight that new knowledge could be uncovered by connecting disparate fields of knowledge. "The system is not organized to cope with combinations [of scientific specialties]," he wrote in his seminal 1986 paper proposing the connection between fish oil and Raynaud's. "Important relationships might be escaping our notice."

Swanson's experience reveals how knowledge is often hidden in plain sight. If A (fish oil) is related to B (blood flow) and B is related to C (Raynaud's symptoms), then there may be a potential relationship between A and C. The challenge, then, if the connections exist in the data, is to find them in a systematic way.

Swanson and a psychiatry professor, Neil Smalheiser, eventually developed a computer program called Arrowsmith that plucked out these needle-like hypotheses from the haystack of medical research databases, with a focus on theories generated out of links between disparate specialties. Swanson later hypothesized a relationship between magnesium deficiency and migraine headaches that was also supported by subsequent clinical research. Swanson called his approach a "stimulus to scientific discovery," acknowledging that there is a big difference between proposing a hypothesis and actually proving it. But it was still an important step for scientific breakthroughs.

Where cross-disciplinary hypotheses once sprang out of idiosyncratic passions and individual experiences—say, Velcro's Swiss inventor getting plant burs (seeds or fruit with hooks) stuck on his pants while hunting and theorizing that their structure might be worth copying in plastic—they can now also emerge from clever mining of data.

Swanson may not have used machine learning to automate his discoveries, but his story also provides an insight into the trade-off between expert systems and machine learning. Expert systems are restricted to the wisdom of experts, wisdom that will, by definition, never fall into the realm of "undiscovered knowledge." We have already seen that learning from data can tap into tacit knowledge that people have but cannot easily articulate. In addition, it can also tap into undiscovered knowledge hidden in data—knowledge that scientists might not have *dis*covered yet but that machine learning and other efforts to mine the data might help *un*cover.

———

The trade-offs between predictability and resilience are not unique to algorithmic decision making. Arguably, there are important lessons to be learned about their respective strengths and shortcomings from even the oldest decision-making systems in human history. No, not flipping a coin!

Dating back to the eighteenth century BCE, the Code of Hammurabi is among the oldest written texts in human history. What makes an ancient Mesopotamian rule book relevant to a discussion around algorithms? It represents a quintessential codified, predictable decision system. The entire text is a series of if-then rules about how society should be run. The vast majority of the text consists of archaic references to idiosyncratic problems facing the ancient Mesopotamians: "If any one be too lazy to keep his dam in proper condition, and does not so keep it; if then the dam break and all the fields be flooded, then shall he in whose dam the break occurred be sold for money, and the money shall replace the grain which he has caused to be ruined." In other respects, the Code of Hammurabi would be a barbaric and a highly irrelevant guide for the modern times, such as in the case of one of its best-known ethical maxims: "If a man destroy the eye of another man, they shall destroy his eye. If one break a man's bone, they shall break his bone."

Contrast this with another of history's highly important political documents, the United States Constitution, which dates back to the eighteenth century. The central values of this foundational document are self-governance and adaptability; built into its very structure is a system for amending it. The key insight of the Founding Fathers was to provide for a government that would be secure and un-usurpable; at the same time, they were aware that they could not possibly predict the needs of a legal system decades, let alone centuries, into the future. Thomas Jefferson acknowledged as much himself:

> Laws and institutions must go hand in hand with the progress of the human mind. As that becomes more developed, more enlightened, as new discoveries are made, new truths discovered and manners and opinions change, with the change of circumstances, institutions must advance also to keep pace with the times. We might as well require a man to wear still the coat which fitted him when a boy as civilized society to remain ever under the regimen of their barbarous ancestors.

The Founding Fathers knew that adaptability is among the most important predictors of resilience and longevity. And the proof is in the Constitution's longevity: it is now the oldest founding document still in use by a modern state. At the same time, its creators had to give up a lot of control over how the future of the United States would play out in order to ensure its resilience.

The juxtaposition of these two documents vividly illustrates the dynamic driving the predictability-resilience tradeoff: predictable systems, such as the Code of Hammurabi, are useful for a limited time, but are ultimately doomed to obsolescence. Resilient systems, such as the U.S. Constitution, must continuously adapt as new information emerges.

Similarly, a debilitating weakness of predictable, rules-based algorithms is not only that they don't perform well in unforeseen scenarios, but also that they don't learn from their mistakes. Most algorithms benefit from more data, but modern machine learning has a very particular advantage. Because machine learning algorithms can actually change their own structure, the more examples to which they are exposed, the finer-tuned they become. They perform a process of adaptation, tweaking their existing rules based on new evidence. This is analogous to how, in the U.S. judicial system, the outcomes of novel, complex court cases become precedents for future similar ones. The more cases the courts see, the more resilient the system becomes.

———

In 2015, a team headquartered at Carnegie Mellon University set out to study how Google's ad-targeting algorithms affected individual users. The researchers created 1,000 simulated user profiles, half male and half female, and had all of them visit the top one hundred employment websites. Next, they evaluated the types of ads displayed by Google to male versus female profiles. They found an algorithmic bias: even though the female profiles were similar to the male ones in every respect but gender, Google's algorithms showed the females far fewer ads related to high-paying, executive-type jobs. For example, an ad for a career-coaching service for executive positions paying more than $200,000 was shown to 402 out of 500 male profiles and to only 60 out of 500 female ones; the female profiles were instead shown ads for a generic job-posting service.

It's hard to explain definitively how this happened. Was the career-coaching service willing to pay Google more to target its ads to male users? The advertiser denied this, explaining that it merely asked to target candidates who were at least forty-five years old, had executive-level experience, and had an annual income of more than $100,000. A Google staff member brought up another possibility: that advertisers generally target women more often than men. Thus, greater across-the-board competition among advertisers to show ads to women might have led to the career-coaching service winning fewer ad slots, perhaps losing out to companies such as sellers of household products, for example, which are known to prefer advertising to women. But this doesn't explain why the generic job-posting service won more ad slots with female profiles.

Another possibility is that the bias reflects one of the fundamental challenges associated with machine learning and all forms of data-driven analytics. If Google's algorithms use past data on ad clickthrough rates to determine how best to target ads in the future, they may draw false conclusions. If the ad was shown to stay-at-home moms who were not looking for a job, for example, then the algorithm would incorrectly learn that women, in general, don't respond to ads for high-paying jobs and would consequently stop displaying such ads to them. Or maybe women do click on the ad—perhaps even more often than men—but if they are even more likely to click on other ads, they will be served those ads instead.

Or maybe the algorithm simply reflects a reality of today's job market. "Imagine Google starts serving these ads equally initially, [and] more male users start clicking on this ad," explains Anupam Datta, one of the study's authors. "Since Google's machine learning algorithms are trying to optimize the clickthrough rate to serve the ad to people more likely to click on it, they'll start serving more of those ads to males."

If so, the algorithm simply reflects the fact that women as a group don't respond as well as men to ads for executive jobs and therefore are less efficient targets for the ad. Can we, therefore, say that the algorithm is biased? "I guess that depends upon your definition, but I would find it concerning whatever you call it," says another of the study's authors, Michael Tschantz, a senior researcher at the International Computer Science Institute in Berkeley. It's easy to understand the nature of Tschantz's concern: if the world we live in has a "bias" wherein women, on average, aren't interested in high-paying jobs, and machines learn from this world, machines will target women less often or less intently. The result will be a self-fulfilling prophecy.

As we discussed in Part One, algorithmic biases arise in many other settings. Credit card companies use online behavioral data—which websites we visit, what kinds of videos we watch, and which products we click on—to make inferences about our income and likely financial behavior. Such information is then used to craft the particular offers and promotions shown on various websites. This practice has raised concerns about *steering*—a term for the illegal practice of guiding minority groups toward less-advantageous credit cards. As in the Google ads example, steering may be completely unintentional, but it is clearly undesirable. Algorithms for policing crime, college admissions, insurance marketing, and hiring that rely on machine learning techniques are all subject to the same issues of fairness.

When we ask machines to learn from Big Data, it is hard to predict precisely what kinds of biases they might pick up. Some have suggested that the solution is to deemphasize Big Data and instead focus on "better data"—that is, to carefully curate "clean" datasets and learn from them. While that approach may work in some situations, I don't think it's a viable path to machine intelligence. Programmers can carefully craft highly sophisticated algorithms for most tasks, but as long as these algorithms are working on small datasets, they will usually lose to simple machine learning algorithms armed with Big Data. In 2001, researchers at Microsoft compared the effectiveness of multiple machine learning algorithms trained on text from news articles and books for a language-understanding task. Each algorithm had to choose the correct word to use in a sentence given a set of confusing alternatives (things such as "principal" versus "principle" or "then" versus "than"). They found that even their poorest-performing algorithm armed with a large training dataset of (say) a billion words comfortably beat the best algorithm with access to a small dataset of (say) 250,000 words. It's what computer scientist Peter Norvig calls "the unreasonable effectiveness of data."

Big Data, with all its messiness, is here to stay.*

———

If these problems—the inevitable trade-offs between quantity and the quality of data—worry you, then the modern world of algorithms has an answer. But the solution pushes our predictability-resilience paradox to a point of extreme tension.

Remember Google's champion-beating AlphaGo software? It was trained partly on past moves by human Go players, partly by playing itself millions of times. The newest iteration of the software doesn't bother with studying human moves; instead, its

———

*The amazing success of Big Data has meant that the term is overused and abused by many. Companies routinely advertise their products as Big Data solutions independent of whether there is any data or machine intelligence powering them. Entrepreneurs whose products touch some data, however small the dataset or however limited the touchpoint, pitch their venture as a Big Data or AI startup. It's created what I call a "my data is bigger than yours" culture in the industry.

entire training dataset is self-generated. That's right: it doesn't tap into Big Data; rather, it *creates* Big Data. The software, armed with basic rules about the legal moves allowed in Go, plays millions of games against itself. Next, it analyzes those games to figure out which moves helped and which ones hurt.

Imagine a child creeping into his grandfather's attic, finding a dusty old box containing a Go board, the game pieces, and a yellowing copy of the rules, and teaching himself how to play. And then becoming a world champion without having a coach or even observing anyone else playing the game. AlphaGo Zero, as the newer version of the Go-playing software has been christened, did just that. In a matter of weeks, from teaching itself the game and practicing its self-taught moves, it won a 100-match tournament against the older AlphaGo (a version, remember, that had studied games played by expert human players). In fact, AlphaGo Zero won resoundingly: 100–0.

Learning from cleanly labeled training data is referred to as *supervised learning*—for example, learning to recognize objects from a training dataset of labeled images. According to computer scientist Andrew Ng, most of the economic value created from machine learning has been through supervised learning. Learning from data generated by an algorithm itself via exploration is referred to as *reinforcement learning*. Algorithms such as AlphaGo Zero simply explore different actions and learn whether those actions lead to better performance.

While reinforcement learning might skirt the problem of messy or biased data, other problems arise. Supervised learning at least limits the set of possible system behaviors to those encountered in the past. Reinforcement learning opens up the possibility of all kinds of new actions or behaviors. And if that approach becomes more pervasive, unpredictability will rise to a whole new level. It is no surprise, then, that many commentators used the word "alien" to describe the moves made by AlphaGo Zero, one Go enthusiast going so far as to call AlphaGo Zero's style of play as "Go from an alternate dimension."

There are no easy answers for any of these scenarios, but it is worth pointing out the beginning of a solution: redundant algorithmic systems, in which multiple approaches are simultaneously employed. Despite the appeal of machine learning, the motion-planning software of self-driving cars may eventually rely on multiple systems, some of which may continue to be rules-based systems that are manually coded by programmers. If the machine learning system becomes confused about a road sign, a set of rules might kick in. This approach might not sound revolutionary—in the evolution of Google's Go-playing bots, it is several generations behind the autodidact phenom AlphaGo Zero. But the use of rules-based approaches to at least set some boundaries for system behavior will be necessary as long as we cannot predict or anticipate how machine learning algorithms might respond to a wide range of situations.

Another solution to the unpredictability of machine learning systems has become one of the hottest areas in AI research: explainable, or *interpretable*, machine learning. How do we build machine learning systems that can explain their decisions—

systems that can, for example, win Go games through "eerie" moves, but walk us through their reasoning? This is a theme I will discuss in a later chapter on transparency.

But first let me turn to an idea that has gripped me for the past several years: the notion that modern algorithms might be best understood through a lens from human psychology—in part because we humans are their creators.

6.

The Psychology
of Algorithms

"Nature or nurture," said the professor. "Whichever way, the parents are to blame!"

François Lelord, *Hector and the Search for Happiness*

Humans are inscrutable. Infinitely unpredictable. This is what makes them dangerous.

Daniel H. Wilson, *Robopocalypse*

We now know how algorithms work. But what does that tell us about why they go rogue? Why did Microsoft's Tay behave so offensively when XiaoIce worked so well? Why did a recidivism algorithm used in U.S. courts show racial bias even though race was not a variable used by the algorithm? And why do social news-feed algorithms create echo chambers when they are supposed to democratize information and create a global village?

Is there a systematic way to think about algorithmic "behavior"?

To answer these questions, let's pretend to be an algorithm shrink. But before we do so, it might not hurt to consult human shrinks and ask them how exactly to study behavior. My brother is a psychiatrist, so that could be a good place to start, right? Wrong. It's never a good idea to consult your own brother, even on something that is his subject-matter expertise. Whatever the topic of discussion, it will end up with a reminder of the time you intentionally broke his tennis racquet as an eight-year-old. So, instead, I consult with several of my colleagues at the University of Pennsylvania. One of them tells me that the most important construct for understanding human behavior is "nature versus nurture," and points me to several recent research papers.

As I catch up on the literature, I recall that the origins of human temperament and behavior have long been debated among philosophers and scientists. Earlier civilizations developed beliefs about the supernatural to explain individual differences. Consider the Babylonian creation of the zodiac signs: Virgos are destined to be analytical, kind, and dedicated, but be careful around the ambitious and frugal Taurus. Plato later asserted that human intelligence and character stemmed from inherited traits; his student Aristotle, however, contended that education and experiences were more influential.

The nature versus nurture debate continued to give rise to controversy for centuries. In *An Essay Concerning Human Understanding*, the English philosopher John Locke argued that at birth, humans were akin to a "blank slate," and that their subsequent behaviors were shaped purely by perception and experience. Darwin's work on the theory of evolution helped popularize the notion that the environment influences both behavior and physical attributes over time, by selecting which heritable characteristics are successful.

At around the same time as Darwin's studies, the late Romantics wrote of nature as an all-encompassing force that was the source of all good in the world. In their eyes, men were born pure, and it was only in the trenches of a corrupt society that they lost their innocence. "Come forth into the light of things, / Let nature be your teacher," wrote Wordsworth. Mary Shelley described her creation, Frankenstein's monster, as "benevolent and good; misery made [it] a fiend."

In the early twentieth century, anthropologist Franz Boas argued that several factors, both biological and environmental, were equally and independently responsible for human development. In the years following the First World War, psychologist John Watson argued that cultural influences completely dominated any predisposed behavioral traits. Soon after the Second World War, in what appeared to be a never-ending seesaw in the nature-nurture debate, the idea that genes determined human character and behavior again started to dominate.

By the 1980s advances in psychology and genetics enabled researchers to empirically answer the nature versus nurture question. Today researchers believe that human behavior is attributable to both our genes and environmental influences. Genetics can predispose someone toward alcoholism or mental disorders such as schizophrenia, but genes alone can't fully explain behavior. Environmental factors, such as the habits of parents and friends, also have a clear influence on alcoholism, and environmental factors such as viral infections or poor nutrition can influence the onset of schizophrenia.

The twin forces of nature and nurture also help to explain the behavior of algorithms. The logic of early computer algorithms was fully programmed; their behavior was therefore completely determined by their human creators. Modern algorithms, in contrast, acquire significant chunks of their logic from real-world data. Much as a child observes and learns from her environment, modern algorithms learn how to drive cars and chat with people by "observing" humans doing the same tasks. The data from which they learn is their "environment."

Accordingly, the behavior of modern algorithms can be described in terms of the manner in which they are programmed (their "genetic code" or nature) and the data to which they are exposed (their nurture). But before we attempt to understand how each drives algorithmic behavior, let's return to human behavior and see what a century of research on nature versus nurture has taught us.

———

We now know that nature and nurture both matter, but how do we know how much each of them matters, and how does that vary for different kinds of behavioral traits? These questions are not just philosophical considerations: the answers are important to psychologists, to policymakers, and to parents, among others, because without them, we would not understand how to intervene and address behavioral problems.

Researchers often use studies of twins to answer these questions, because twins share a large set of genes and often grow up under similar, if not identical, environmental influences. Twins therefore offer a unique opportunity to assess the impact of genes and environments on behavioral traits and physical attributes.

There are two main groups into which twins can be segmented: identical twins and fraternal twins. Identical twins have the exact same set of genes and are therefore governed by the exact same genetic blueprint, whereas fraternal twins share only half of their genes, on average, with each other. According to Nancy Segal, a professor of psychology and the director of the Twin Studies Center at California State University, Fullerton, comparing these twin types against each other provides the chance to isolate the impact of genes, since both sets of twins are likely to have been raised in similar environments, but fraternal twins bear less genetic similarity than identical ones. Segal also points to another rare prospect in studying twins—identical twins who have been raised apart, which she terms "the ultimate gold standard in twin studies," because they share only their genes but not their environment.

Consider the story of two pairs of identical twins who were born at the same time in a hospital in Colombia. Somehow, one brother from each pair was swapped at the hospital. As a result, two sets of unrelated individuals grew up together believing they were fraternal twins. Carlos and Jorge were raised in a city with a lot of opportunities, while William and Wilber were raised in a rural area without electricity or a school within five miles. These different environments clearly affected the course of their lives. For example, as an adult, Jorge worked at an engineering firm. His identical twin, William, was forced to drop out of school and took a job as a butcher. The twins eventually reunited twenty-five years after they were born, when a colleague of Jorge's encountered William at a butcher shop. Segal, who studied the two pairs of twins, found that even though they had been raised in dramatically different environments, each pair of identical twins still bore many similarities in their personalities. For example, Jorge and William were more organized and had a positive temperament, while Carlos and Wilber chased girls and were more emotional.

Segal mentions an additional group: virtual twins, unrelated siblings who are born to entirely different sets of parents but come into a family at the same time and the same age—for example, children who are adopted together as babies. Virtual twins are almost a perfect reverse situation from that of identical twins raised apart. "These are precious kinships, because they give us a pure estimate of environmental effects. They share no genes in common," says Segal. Research shows that virtual twins, as they age, grow less and less alike as their genetic potential develops and they are free from their parents' influence.

Together, these varying conditions and groupings of twins give researchers the range of variation necessary to isolate the impact of genetic and environmental factors on physical development, behavior, and attitudes. The results suggest that neither side of the nature versus nurture debate is in itself correct. Segal found that the IQ levels of identical twins are highly matched, suggesting that about 70 percent of the variation in intelligence in a population comes from the genetic pool. Generally speaking, personality is influenced 50 percent by genes and 50 percent by the environment. About 30 percent of the variation in job satisfaction is attributable to genes. In contrast, for physical attributes such as height and weight, Segal indicates that 90 percent of the variation in a population stems from genes.

What might twin research teach us about the behavior of algorithms? One way to identify the relative importance of nature and nurture in them is to study similar algorithms operating in different data environments, or different algorithms operating in similar data environments. Microsoft's launches of XiaoIce and Tay offers one such opportunity. Both chatbots were developed by the same company using similar approaches to language processing and understanding. They are effectively fraternal twins who grew up in very different social networks. That one was warm and loving and the other was racist and sexist shows how much nurture matters with modern machine learning–based algorithms.

Microsoft's XiaoIce learned how to chat affectionately and inspire warmth and love by observing people communicate in that manner. Tay learned how to be bigoted and prejudiced from human conversation as well. Differences in cultural norms—for example, the big-brother-is-watching dynamic of Chinese social networks—mean that the environment in which XiaoIce learned how to converse was very different from the chaotic, anything-goes Twitter environment where Tay operated.

Does that mean that modern algorithms' behavior is completely driven by their nurture? Roman Yampolsky, an AI researcher, suggests that the problem with Tay was that Microsoft had not programmed it with an understanding of what behavior was inappropriate. Perhaps its code needed some tweaking in order for it to thrive in a difficult environment like Twitter.

In March 2017 Microsoft launched Zo, another chatbot. Unlike Tay, Zo had been explicitly programmed to avoid political rhetoric or unsuitable behavior. That Zo's responses were explicitly curtailed by its programmers helped avoid the missteps that plagued Tay within minutes of its launch. Still, a British tabloid captured the following conversation:

> USER: What do you think about healthcare?
> ZO: The far majority practise it peacefully but the quaran is very violent.

Even Microsoft's extensive testing of Zo following Tay's public failure couldn't prevent such missteps. Clearly, fine-tuning the nature and nurture of modern algorithms to create resilient but well-behaved models will continue to be a delicate matter.

Microsoft's experiences with Tay and Zo offer a valuable lesson about rogue algorithmic behavior: sometimes the problem with algorithms may be that they are simply hanging out with bad data. Or as Yuan Zhang, the avid XiaoIce user I mentioned in the Introduction, put it following the Tay disaster: "Tay is the child of all her users. We should become better parents."

We now have a framework for deconstructing algorithmic systems into three fundamental components: the underlying data on which they are trained, the logic of the algorithms themselves, and the ways in which users interact with the algorithms. Each of these components feeds into the others. Algorithms learn from or act on data and make suggestions or decisions on our behalf. Users in turn interact with algorithmic recommendations, and these interactions create the next generation of data for the algorithms. Together, the three components determine the intended and unintended consequences of algorithmic systems.

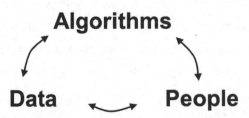

The results of algorithmic systems can be attributed to their underlying data, their mathematical logic, and the ways in which people interact with their decisions and suggestions

Social media sites such as Facebook and Twitter and search engines such as Google are increasingly prominent sources of information and news for the general public. However, many critics have raised concerns that the use of personalization algorithms by these firms is effectively fragmenting society: because algorithms at large tech companies learn our preferences over time, the more we use these tools, the less likely it is that we encounter content that reflects a perspective different from our own. The result is a "filter bubble" in which we all have our own narrow information base.

Echo chambers are obviously problematic, as social discourse suffers without a shared body of information. But are algorithms the primary drivers of online echo chambers? And how do we quantify their role vis-à-vis the other factors such as data and user interactions?

In studies from 2010 and 2014, my research group at Wharton evaluated a subject a bit less divisive than political fragmentation: music listening patterns. More than 1,700 iTunes users were shown personalized content recommendations, while a comparable group of users did not receive such recommendations. The analysis measured the overlap in songs consumed by users—the extent to which two randomly selected users consumed the same music. If people were fragmenting due to personalized recommendations, the overlap would presumably decrease in the group that received them.

In fact, we found the opposite was true: after listeners were exposed to recommendation algorithms, overlap in music consumption rose. This increase occurs for two reasons. First, users simply listen to more music when an algorithm finds relevant selections for them. And if two users listen to, say, twice as many songs as they had before, then their chance of consuming the same songs also increases. Second, algorithmic recommendations help users explore and branch into new interests, thereby increasing the likelihood of overlap with others. In short, we didn't find evidence for an echo chamber.

It could be argued that political content differs from other forms of media. For example, people are less likely to hold extreme views or become polarized over music than political ideologies. Furthermore, news feeds on social networks such as Facebook operate differently than the personalized recommendations you might see on YouTube or Google News. Would our results be replicated on social media as well? And with political news consumption?

A 2015 study conducted by researchers at Facebook offers an answer. They evaluated the news feeds of 10.1 million active Facebook users in the United States who self-reported their political ideology as either conservative, moderate, or liberal. The researchers wanted to analyze how the social network's algorithms influenced its users' exposure to diverse perspectives. To do so, they calculated what proportion of the news stories that appeared in these users' news feeds were "crosscutting"—defined as having a perspective other than the users' own (for example, a liberal reading a news story with a primarily conservative perspective). The researchers identified three factors that influence the extent to which we see crosscutting news: first, who our friends are and what news stories they share; second, among all the news stories shared by friends, which are selected by the news-feed algorithm to appear in front of us; and third, which of those news stories we click on. These three factors align nicely with the framework proposed above. A Facebook user's friends and the articles those friends share are the data. The news-feed system that takes that input and chooses which articles to display is the algorithm. And users deciding which of those articles to click through to and read are the people.

By systematically comparing the extent to which exposure to crosscutting news is affected by each step in this process, the researchers were able to quantify the degree to which each factor affects the ideological diversity of news consumption on Facebook. If the second step—the news-feed algorithm itself— was the primary driver of the echo chamber, the specific logic of the filtering algorithms would be to blame. If the first or third steps were more responsible for creating a filter bubble, it would suggest that either the data or the ways in which we interact with algorithmic suggestions was more significant than the algorithms themselves.

The researchers report that if we acquired our news media from a randomly selected group of Facebook users, nearly 45 percent of news seen by liberals and 40 percent seen by conservatives on the site would be crosscutting. But we don't get our news suggestions from a randomly selected group; we get them from our friends. As a result, the researchers found that only 24 percent of news stories shared by liberals' friends and about 35 percent of stories shared by conservatives' friends were cross-cutting. Clearly, the like-mindedness of our Facebook friends traps us in an echo chamber.

The news-feed algorithm further selects which of the friends' news stories to show you, based on your prior interaction with friends. Because we tend to engage more with like-minded friends and websites that reflect our own ideology, the news-feed algorithm further reduces the proportion of crosscutting news stories to 22 percent for liberals and 34 percent for conservatives (see figure below). In other words, Facebook's algorithm worsens the echo chamber, but not by much.

Finally, which of the news stories that we have been fed do we click on? The researchers find that 21 percent of news stories that liberals click and 30 percent that conservatives do are cross-cutting. We seem to prefer reading news items that are likely to reinforce rather than challenge our existing views, but again, the effect of this step is modest relative to that of who our Facebook friends are.

The authors conclude that the digital echo chamber is driven by the actions of users—whom we connect with online and which stories we click on—rather than the choices that the news-feed algorithm makes on our behalf.

Given that this research was conducted in-house by Facebook's social scientists, critics may be skeptical. However, their

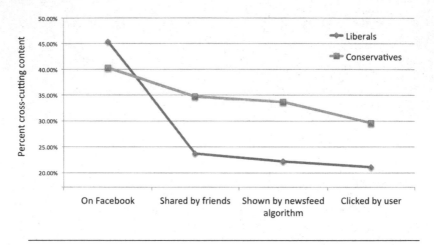

The drop in crosscutting content is driven mainly by the like-mindedness of our friends. Graph based on figures shared in Facebook paper.

results are consistent with those of another recent study conducted at Stanford University that analyzed the browsing histories of 50,000 individuals in the United States. The researchers found that the vast majority of news articles consumed by individuals is determined simply by their visits to the homepages of their favorite news websites rather than by social media filtering algorithms.

How do we reconcile findings that absolve algorithms with our own experience on social media websites? To better understand the phenomenon, my student Alex Miller and I created virtual worlds in which we simulated algorithmic news recommendations and consumer choice. The goal was to look more holistically at all three components of an algorithmic system:

the algorithm, the input datasets, and the users. One of our simulated worlds was highly polarized: people belonged to one of two groups with extreme political views, and there was very little overlap between these groups. The second world, which we called a global village, was one in which the two groups did not differ greatly in their political preferences. People made decisions on which news stories to read based on these preferences. Their choices provided the input datasets for algorithms that could then recommend additional news stories to readers.

We created two news personalization algorithms for each virtual world. The first was a commonly used design that finds people with similar prior choices and recommends the most popular news stories they consume. ("People like you also read . . .") A second algorithm recommended a full range of stories that were consumed by people with similar prior choices rather than focusing on the most popular story they consumed. In short, we evaluated two different algorithms and two different input datasets (generated by two different user preference structures). We then assessed the level of polarization in these worlds by measuring the extent to which users in one group also consumed stories that were consumed by users in the other group. A shared information base is, after all, an important bedrock for positive political discourse.

We found that algorithms do indeed have a role to play in determining how polarized we are. For a given set of users, some algorithms will increase polarization, while others can decrease it. This suggests that the specific algorithms that platform designers choose to deploy can indeed contribute to the filter bubble. On the other hand, we also found that the same algorithm can both increase and decrease polarization, depending on the underlying preferences of users. Our modified algorithm increased polarization relative to the traditional personalization algorithm in an already polarized world. However, it reduced polarization in the global village. It seems there is no one-size-fits-all solution to mitigating polarization on social media. A particular algorithm may exacerbate the echo chamber effect in one context while mitigating it in another. Another way of viewing the results of our research is simply that data and algorithms interact in complex ways.

Even in a simplistic, simulated world in which only a small number of factors varied, we observed complex interactions between data and algorithms. In real-world environments, the algorithms are more opaque, the datasets more massive, and users exhibit more-complex patterns of behavior. All of these factors only increase the complexity of the situation.

As we engineer our algorithmic systems, the algorithms themselves certainly deserve a high degree of scrutiny. But it is important to not forget the role of other contributing elements. As our study has shown, the same algorithm can have dramatically different effects depending on the context in which it is applied, and the same input data can have varying results depending on the algorithm that is acting on the data.

And then there's the human factor. A team of researchers in Finland and Qatar tried to design an algorithm that recommends crosscutting news articles to people. The researchers found that simply exposing people to information they disagree with was ineffective. Instead, it was better to show crosscutting information that wasn't too far from people's existing viewpoints. Starting with moderate perspectives that offered some shared viewpoints was more effective in bridging polarized users. Kiran Garimella, the lead researcher, told a *Slate* journalist that one important insight from the work was a broad one that we need to acknowledge as we attend to the unintended consequences of algorithmic decisions: "This is definitely not a computer science problem in itself. . . . This is really an interdisciplinary problem. You need a psychologist, you need a social scientist to understand how people behave."

———

We are now at a moment of scientific consensus that neither genetics nor our environment alone is responsible for our traits; they are a product not just of both but also of complex interactions between the two—a concept referred to as Nature x Nurture. For example, the onset of certain genetic diseases such as phenylketonuria (a build-up of an amino acid in the blood, potentially leading to brain damage) is known to be affected by diet. Similarly, exposure to sunlight has a much greater impact on skin cancer risk for fair-skinned people than dark-skinned ones. In both these cases, specific combinations of genes and environments increase the risk of diseases.

Further, nature and nurture aren't the independent entities they've long been viewed as. All of us have genetic predispositions that lead us to gravitate toward certain people and activities—even the jobs we seek may be influenced by genes. In short, our genetics are partially responsible for creating our environment. Psychologist Segal points out that identical twins raised apart are as similar as they are not just because of their genes but also because they gravitate toward similar people and things in their respective environments: "Our genes do not dictate what to do. But they do predispose us."

I have arrived at a similar conclusion about algorithms—namely, that the social media echo chamber (and, arguably, all unintended consequences of algorithmic decisions) is a result of a complex cocktail of the nature and nurture of algorithms and the manner in which people interact with them. While each of the components—data, algorithms, and people—plays a significant role in determining the outcomes of algorithmic systems, the sum is often greater than the parts, with the complex interactions between the various components having the greatest impact of all.

Solving the unintended consequences of algorithms will require us to evaluate these complex interactions. I next turn to them and highlight the component to which I have paid the least attention so far—the people who use algorithms to inform their decisions.

Part Three

TAMING
THE CODE

7.

In Algorithms We Trust

Never trust anything that can think for itself *if you can't
see where it keeps its brain.*

J. K. Rowling, *Harry Potter and the Chamber of Secrets*

O n a beautiful Saturday afternoon in May 2016, on a
sunny stretch of road in northern Florida, Joshua Brown,
a forty-year-old entrepreneur and technology enthusiast
from northeastern Ohio, was sitting behind the wheel of his
Tesla Model S sedan. He'd just spent a week with family at Dis-
ney World, they had all said goodbye that morning, and he was
now driving to a business meeting for a company he had started
five years earlier, to help bring internet access to rural areas.

At about twenty minutes before 5:00 p.m., Brown's car was
zipping along U.S. highway 27A when a semi carrying blueber-
ries in the opposite direction pulled into a left turn lane and
then crossed the road ahead of him. Reports suggest that the

truck driver ought to have waited for Brown to pass, but there was still sufficient time for Brown to slow down.

The Tesla, which Brown had put into self-driving Autopilot mode, failed to register the white truck against the bright sky. Brown himself failed to take control and engage the brakes. The car crashed into the side of the truck-trailer at seventy-four miles an hour, then continued under it until hitting a utility pole, spinning, and finally coming to rest. Brown, investigators believe, was killed almost instantly upon the Tesla's impact with the truck.

Brown's death is the first known fatality in a car operating in self-driving mode, and it got a lot of attention in the technology and automobile worlds. Some media commentators and industry analysts had already faulted Tesla for including Autopilot in its cars because the technology was still in beta mode. Others had criticized the company for not doing more to ensure that drivers are actively in control of their vehicles while Autopilot is engaged. Less than a month before the accident, Elon Musk, Tesla's founder, had promoted a video Brown himself had made of a different Tesla Autopilot experience, wherein the car successfully noted and avoided a truck pulling ahead of it. Now, after the fatal accident, Musk found himself defending Autopilot as a lifesaving technology that, when used correctly, would reduce the overall number of vehicle fatalities.

Most experts agree. In more than 90 percent of conventional crashes, human error is to blame. According to some estimates, self-driving cars could save up to 1.5 million lives just in the United States and close to 50 million lives globally in the next fifty years. Yet in an April 2018 poll, 50 percent of the respondents said they believed autonomous cars were less safe than human drivers. After the Tesla crash, consumers were apoplectic. "This dangerous technology should be banned. Get it off the road. The public streets are not a place to experiment with unproven self-driving systems," wrote a San Franciscan commenting in a discussion forum. Clearly, people viewed Brown's death as less an anomaly than a harbinger of things to come. If robots were going to take over our roads, they deserved serious scrutiny first. The National Transportation Safety Board, which is responsible for investigating airplane and train accidents, among other things, launched an inquiry.

The NTSB published its report in June 2017. Among the findings were that Brown had used the car's Autopilot mode on an inappropriate road; Tesla's manuals had instructed that it be used only on highways "where access is limited by entry and exit ramps," not where a truck might make a left turn across two lanes of oncoming traffic. Moreover, where Tesla stated that a "fully attentive driver" should oversee the car's actions even in Autopilot, Brown had been inattentive for at least thirty seconds before the crash. He may have been so because he had successfully used the Autopilot multiple times in the past and had begun to become more comfortable with the feature. The report's authors included advice to car manufacturers: "Until automated vehicle systems mature, driver engagement remains integral to the automated driving system." It is the carmakers' responsibility, they said, to build systems that ensure drivers remain engaged.

────────

At the same time the NTSB investigation was being conducted, executives at a company that helps people invest their savings were getting a very different message from institutions and individuals alike: keep human hands *off* the wheel (figuratively speaking).

Betterment, launched in 2010, was the brainchild of a thirty-year-old named Jonathan Stein, whose idea was to create a service that "took investing best practices and applied them automatically." That is, don't pick stock and don't meddle, because you're not going to be able to beat the market; instead, use an algorithm to steer your investments down a safe and profitable path. Automating the investment process would also help lower the fees and make investment management services accessible to many more people. Stein's pitch attracted some 400 investors at its introduction, growing to 10,000 in a year, and to 270,000 by late 2017. In July 2017, a month after the NTSB's Tesla crash report was published, Betterment became the first of the independent "robo-advisers" to break the $10 billion mark for assets under management. By the end of 2017, independent robo-advisers such as Betterment and Wealthfront, as well as Vanguard and other traditional investment companies, were collectively managing more than $200 billion in assets through automated investment platforms.

People hopped onto this particular bus *because* a robot was driving, not despite the fact. As one blogger put it, "One of the features of Betterment is that their computers spend all day looking at the stock market while you are off doing other things . . . and I am coming to realize that this feature works much better than I had expected." Moreover, its customers were not just the millennials that Stein and his team might have originally had in mind: a third of them are over fifty, according to the company.

For some time now, we've been relying on algorithms in many different contexts—from low-risk activities, such as deciding what to watch on Netflix, to high-stakes situations, such as dating or investing our savings. This strange discrepancy between our current acceptance of recommendation algorithms and robo-advisers and our skepticism regarding self-driving cars raises a crucial question: Why do we trust algorithms in some cases, but not in others? And why do some of us trust them more than others?

I posed these questions in an article for the *Harvard Business Review* after the Tesla crash, and the commenters came up with several explanations, which researchers in the area are also exploring. One hypothesized that we don't trust driverless cars because algorithmic driving hasn't proven to be superior to human drivers. This makes logical sense: Unless a machine has demonstrated that it is, in fact, better, why choose it over our relatively trustworthy selves? And yet initial research has shown that existing technology *is* safer than most human drivers. While the death of a driver in a traffic accident is a tragedy, early empirical evidence does support the fact that autonomous cars, on average, are more attentive and reliable than human drivers.

And the superiority of algorithms over human decision making is not restricted to autonomous cars. In 1996, two psychologists at the University of Minnesota, William Grove and Paul Meehl, published a meta-analysis of 136 studies that provided 617 direct comparisons between algorithmic and human predictions of health-related phenomena. They included only cases where the human expert had an amount of information equal to or greater than what the machine had. The algorithms outperformed the humans in 64 studies, the two methods were considered equal in another 64 studies, and the clinician outperformed the algorithm in only 8 cases. Yet "despite 66 years of consistent research findings in favor of the actuarial [or mechanical, or algorithmic] method," Grove and Meehl write, "most professionals continue to use a subjective, clinical judgment approach when making predictive decisions." Beyond clinical settings, research has shown that algorithms and statistical models beat humans at college admissions and job screening, both of which rely on the fairly complex task of forecasting future performance and success, but the adoption of algorithms remains quite limited in all these settings.

Another explanation is that while we may accept the fact that algorithms outperform humans on average, we continue to believe that we are better than the average. This would explain why we are willing to accept robo-advisers such as Betterment and happily board planes piloted largely by computers; after all, algorithms are replacing some other human decision maker in these cases. But we don't want to hand over the keys to our own car because we're confident that we're not that reckless driver who gets distracted by a phone call or takes turns too quickly.

This conviction is in fact rooted in a well-documented phenomenon that social psychologists call the *better-than-average effect*. In a survey of approximately a million students who took the SAT college admissions test in 1976, 70 percent placed themselves above the median (i.e. in the top 50 percent) in leadership skills, and 85 percent placed themselves above median in their ability to get along with others. This bias isn't confined to students. A survey of faculty revealed that 68 percent rated themselves in the top 25 percent in teaching ability. And closer to our theme of driving, in a survey of driving skills, 93 percent of responders in the United States rated themselves in the top 50 percent.*

---

*The same study found that 69 percent of Swedish survey responders (as compared to 93 percent in the U.S. sample) rated themselves in the top 50 percent. The better-than-average effect is probably more pronounced in the U.S. than in other countries. In fact, if you had surveyed my friends and me before our college entrance exam in India in the mid-1990s, you might have seen a "worse-than-average" effect in which 90% of us thought we were below average. Our educational system

Jennifer Logg, a researcher at the University of California, Berkeley, performed a study that confirmed that people compare themselves more favorably to algorithms than they do other people. She asked participants to rank U.S. states according to the number of airline passenger departures, making estimates based on information such as the number of major airports in each state, census population, and median household income. After they made their predictions, one group of subjects was asked to accept either another participant's estimate or the estimate of an algorithm. They overwhelmingly preferred the algorithm. A second group was asked to either accept the algorithm's estimate or stick with their own. These subjects also preferred the algorithm, but not as overwhelmingly as the first group. We do trust algorithms over humans, it seems—particularly when that human is someone else.

Another suggestion I received in response to my article was that whether we trust algorithms is dependent not on their performance relative to humans but rather on the actual stakes involved: the greater the cost of a poor decision, the less humans are willing to trust machines. After all, a poor movie recommendation results only in the loss of several hours and a few dollars. The stakes are much higher with life savings and autonomous vehicles. And yet even here, people's willingness to trust robo-

---

had a unique way of shaming us into working hard. But I should perhaps better take that issue to a therapist than to my readers.

advisers and planes on autopilot is not consistent with this theory: these are high-stakes scenarios, but we still yield to algorithm control.

Let's consider another hypothesis that a commenter proposed, one based on the complexity of the given task. This person argued that we have trouble trusting algorithms because we believe that humans, unlike algorithms, can learn and improve with experience. And since programmers can't anticipate and preprogram every type of situation that might be encountered, we trust that the human brain is better at handling new and unanticipated scenarios. This argument, however, doesn't take into account that machine learning algorithms can, in fact "learn" and therefore deal with novel situations much as humans do.

Another interesting idea suggested by psychologist Robyn Dawes is that people might be reluctant to adopt algorithms in some settings because they view doing so as dehumanizing. For example, when decisions about whom to hire, retain, or promote are made through algorithmic number crunching, it often feels as if "people have been reduced to numbers," and the ethicality of such choices might make some uneasy. This seems a perfectly valid argument, though I have yet to see any empirical evidence to support it.

As the above examples show, the question of what drives trust in algorithms is multifaceted. Ascertaining when and why humans trust machines requires that we accept that, like humans, no two algorithms are alike. There are important ways in which product recommendation algorithms, investment management tools, dating apps, and driverless cars differ. Accounting for these differences is critical to understanding what drives trust in algorithms.

Let's do a quick thought experiment. Write down three decisions for which you would prefer to consult a human over an algorithm. Next, list three decisions for which you would prefer algorithmic over human advice.

The top categories of decisions for which I'd prefer humans over algorithms are those related to my professional life (e.g., identifying new directions for my career) or personal relationships (e.g., which friendships to invest time in). Those for which I'd turn to algorithms include movie or music choices and the stocks or index funds in which to invest. As noted above, existing research also suggests that algorithms for student admissions and job screening often outperform human forecasters, so I might add those to my list, while acknowledging that I have never tried any algorithms for these areas despite being actively involved in both of them.

Are there systematic patterns in the types of decisions we would entrust to algorithms over human advisers (and vice versa)? In one of her earlier studies, Jennifer Logg explored precisely this question, asking subjects to do the same thought experiment presented above. Logg found that her subjects were much more inclined to trust algorithms with estimates and predictions that are objective (that is, those that have correct and verifiable answers, such as which credit card offers the best deals) than with subjective material (such as whether to break up with your girlfriend). Algorithms are commonly seen as robotic, emotionless, and unbiased. It then makes sense that humans are simply unable to reconcile this image of them with the idea that they can offer aid in emotional matters.

Of course, the thought experiment suffers from a flaw: there's no real algorithm to observe in action before we decide whether or not to rely on it. In contrast, our choice to continue depending on Amazon's recommendations or Google's driving directions is based on repeated interactions with these systems. The ability to repeatedly observe an algorithm's performance—both when it does well and when it fails—should surely play a role in our decision to trust them; but how?

Berkeley Dietvorst, Joseph Simmons, and Cade Massey, my colleagues at Wharton, have been looking into the way people react when algorithms make mistakes—in other words, how we respond to algorithms as we experience their functioning over time. In an experiment, subjects were asked to play the role of an MBA admissions officer and were provided with details of student applicants, such as test scores, work experience, and salaries. They were also informed that a statistical model designed to forecast student performance, based on hundreds of past applicants, was available.

In an initial trial run, one group of subjects was allowed to look at the statistical model's performance, and thus saw how well it did and where it made mistakes. Participants in a second group made their own forecasts on student performance and then saw how well they did. Participants in a third group got a chance to observe their own forecasting performance as well as that of the statistical model. Finally, participants in a control group did not have an initial trial run and thus did not see the algorithm's performance.

In the next stage, the subjects were asked to forecast the likely performance of student applicants, either on their own or using the statistical model. The subjects were compensated based on the accuracy of their forecasts. The two groups that observed the statistical model's performance during the trial run turned out to be much less likely than the control group to rely on the model; 65 percent of subjects in the control group picked the algorithm for forecasting, but only about a quarter of students who had previously observed the algorithm selected it. In contrast, subjects who had observed their own forecasting performance during the trial run were just as likely as the control group to rely on their own judgment. This was despite the fact that the model's forecasts were more accurate than those of the human subjects. It seemed the applicants were more forgiving of their own mistakes than those of the algorithm.

In short, people lose confidence in algorithms much more than they do in human forecasters when they observe both make the same mistake.

One interesting thought experiment shared by the authors

illustrates this mind-set perfectly. Imagine that one day on your morning drive to work, you decide to take a shortcut, which you estimate will save you about twenty minutes. However, the new route winds up being congested with traffic, and your travel time is ten minutes longer than usual. You likely shrug the delay off and decide not to take that route again. If a GPS had made the same error, however, you would probably be reluctant to use that device for similar situations in the future. It's clear that we are somehow unable to reconcile the idea of algorithms with the possibility that they can fail, even while accepting that humans are fallible.

That appears to be what happened after Joshua Brown's Tesla crash. "Dying due to your own error is just more acceptable than due to sensor failure. This is why I wouldn't buy [an] autopilot option," wrote one person on Brown's YouTube channel comments. The implication for self-driving car manufacturers and proponents is that the public might rapidly lose trust in the technology if there are enough incidents such as the one involving Joshua Brown's Tesla, however much the technology has been proven to be safer in the aggregate. Further evidence of this emerged in March 2018 when a self-driving vehicle being tested by Uber killed a pedestrian in Tempe, Arizona. A poll in January 2018 had revealed that 36 percent of survey participants considered self-driving cars to be less safe than regular cars driven by humans. The same survey question, administered by the same pollster shortly after the Uber accident, saw the number of skeptics climb to 50 percent.

———

In 1998 the U.S. Food and Drug Administration approved the use of algorithms to help radiologists analyze mammograms for signs of cancer. The practice's popularity subsequently soared: in 2002, fewer than 5 percent of clinics in the nationwide Breast Cancer Surveillance Consortium were using computers to scan images, according to a 2015 study; by 2012, 8 in 10 scans were analyzed with the aid of algorithm-powered machines. The result was a significant uptick in biopsies.

Were the algorithms outperforming their human counterparts, identifying cancerous lesions that even experienced radiologists would have missed? Unfortunately, no. Several studies have shown that while computer-assisted detection put more women under the scalpel, the biopsies often revealed false-positive readings. In fact, the detection of small, invasive breast cancers decreased during the period.

These early algorithms were expert systems based on rules that are often used to train radiologists. These have worked well in many cases, but as I have mentioned earlier, expert systems aren't resilient and often can't handle exceptions to the rules. In contrast, even though budding radiologists learn many rules, as we have seen, much of their work involves pattern recognition that is honed by experience. "Senior doctors don't really think about many of their decisions. They engage in an experience-based form of pattern matching," explains Luke Oakden-Rayner, the Australian radiologist, computer science researcher, and blogger. Such rapid pattern identification requires perception, but expert systems struggle with it.

Deep-learning systems, in contrast, excel at perception and are likely to do better at diagnostic tasks in radiology and dermatology. More-recent iterations are unlikely to suffer from the performance issues that plagued early expert systems, but might the earlier generation's failures discourage the adoption of the new generation of diagnostic tools? The Wharton study suggests that the shortcomings of early systems will have eroded trust among radiologists, and they will need a great deal more convincing before they adopt the much improved deep-learning ones. Such negative initial experiences may well serve as a cautionary note for the premature rollout of algorithmic systems.

There is an additional issue beyond the failures of early expert systems. While the newer machine learning–based algorithms perform better, the hype surrounding them often exceeds their actual abilities. The notion that machine is now besting man in medical fields ranging from oncology to diabetes management is rife among journalists, but the facts do not bear this out.

Ranjani Ramamurthy, a physician who now works on AI applications in healthcare at Microsoft, has examined some of these news stories, as well as the underlying research, and argues that our willingness to jump on the algorithm-as-physician bandwagon stems from a fundamental misunderstanding of doctors' work: "Doctors don't do predictions. They do diagnosis." Referring to a paper about computers outperforming pathologists when it came to predicting lung cancer patients' survival times, she pointed out that "[Pathologists] don't do such predictions. They look at the tissue and they tell you what they see. Most of the time, when you say AI trumps doctors, you have to ask whether it's a task that doctors even do." Citing a study that describes a machine learning algorithm predicting Alzheimer's ten years before the disease set in, Ramamurthy points out that the algorithm used MRI brain scans of patients without symptoms of the disease to make its projections. "This is not the standard of care. Nobody does MRIs to see if one has Alzheimer's before there are any signs or symptoms that bring the patient to the doctor." Doctors usually diagnose Alzheimer's based on actual symptoms, such as forgetfulness. Oakden-Rayner has written extensively on this subject and shares Ramamurthy's skepticism about medical reporting touting AI's triumphs in the medical arena: "They either don't understand medicine, they don't understand AI, or they don't actually compare doctors and machines."

This is not to say that all studies comparing AI against doctors make the same mistake. Researchers from Stanford published an article in *Nature* in early 2017 that described an algorithm trained on a database of 130,000 skin-disease images that diagnosed potentially cancerous skin lesions. Its performance matched that of twenty-one board-certified dermatologists. Ramamurthy highlights the fact that identifying melanoma based on the appearance of skin lesions is a diagnosis that doctors actually make, so it's a big deal if computers can reach par with those doctors.

Algorithms are also reaching par with doctors on other diagnostic tasks, such as the detection of diabetic retinopathy (DR), a leading cause of preventable blindness globally. The disease diminishes quality of life in all the obvious ways, but it also affects its victims' earning potential, often dooming them to poverty. K. Chandrashekhar, founder and chief executive of India-based Forus Health, built a medical device to detect DR. Existing equipment was too expensive to be used by hospitals in India and Africa, so Chandrashekhar and his team developed a more affordable alternative.

Doctors most commonly diagnose diabetic retinopathy by examining pictures of the back of the eye. Interpreting these photographs requires specialized training, but there are seldom qualified doctors present in the subcontinent's small towns and villages. Chandrashekhar's solution is to record the images through his device and upload them to the cloud, allowing doctors in urban centers to examine the photos and diagnose the patient from afar. While this is a brilliant solution, the problem remains that there are few qualified doctors, even in cities, who can assess the images for the millions of at-risk patients around the world. That's why Chandrashekhar and many others in the business of medical diagnosis paid close attention when Google decided to apply itself to this problem. It built a dataset of 128,000 retinal photographs and then paid professional ophthalmologists to grade the images for the presence of DR. The researchers then used the database to train an algorithm at detection; it performed on par with another set of ophthalmologists viewing the photos.

Google's automated ophthalmologist is not an expert system but a machine learning algorithm. And a deep learning one at that. Oakden-Rayner observes, "If it [an algorithm] isn't deep learning, it probably isn't better than a doctor." But deep learning ability alone isn't sufficient. Unlike other systems described in many sensational news accounts, the Google algorithm performs a classification task that doctors carry out. That is where the focus of researchers and media should be—applying algorithms to support decisions that doctors actually make.

But if algorithms do improve at the tasks that doctors actually perform, what will be the future role of physicians? Oakden-Rayner believes that professions such as radiology and pathology, which are highly perceptual in nature, as they involve looking at medical scans or microscopic slides and finding patterns, are most at risk. Speaking at a hospital in 2016, computer scientist Geoff Hinton, one of the godfathers of deep learning, said, "People should stop training radiologists now. It is just completely obvious that within five years, deep learning is going to do better than radiologists." Or, as Oakden-Rayner puts it, the medpocalypse may soon be here for many medical professions.

But others have a more positive view of the future of these fields. Sebastian Thrun, an entrepreneur, innovator, and adjunct professor at Stanford, believes that AI systems will be used to aid, rather than replace, humans. "When you use a phone, you amplify the power of human speech. You cannot shout from New York to California," Thrun told writer Siddhartha Mukherjee, "and yet this rectangular device in your hand allows the human voice to be transmitted across three thousand miles. Did the phone replace the human voice? No, the phone is an augmentation device." Thrun believes automated diagnoses will similarly augment rather than displace radiologists and dermatologists.

There is little doubt that radiology and many other professions are going to be redefined if advanced algorithmic systems are adopted intelligently by their users. But we cannot take user adoption for granted, especially in light of AI's public and trust-sapping failures. If we do, we might be marching toward a world of superhuman diagnostic systems that no doctors are willing to use—or a world of safe and effective driverless cars with no passengers willing to ride in them.

8.

Which Is to Be Master—Algorithm or User?

> "The question is," said Humpty Dumpty, "which is to be master—that's all."
>
> Lewis Carroll, *Through the Looking Glass*

Earlier this year I was browsing through my Facebook news feed when I came across a post by a friend about the unfortunate demise of one of his closest friends from high school. I was greatly moved by his words, and as I sat thinking about the tragic loss of a young life, I scrolled down. Right below that post was a hilarious video of a movie fight scene from the 1970s that had been shared by another friend. The "so bad it's good" sequence helped explain why today's producers hire specialist fight choreographers. Further below was a funny segment from a late-night show. By the time I closed the browser tab about ten minutes later, I realized just how inconsistent the experience had been. I was distraught and emotional one minute and amused and jovial the next. But these emotions, particularly my empathy for my friend's pain, felt disingenuous. The news-feed experience itself was emotionally inconsistent; it didn't mirror a genuine social interaction with a friend. Instead, the experience was more like watching a movie in which a lot of drama had been packed into the time available.

This is by no means the only unusual thing about the way my news feed is organized. Posts by friends about important social and political issues of the day appear to have the same weight as pictures posted by friends at airport business lounges. Posts about sports figures and sporting events of particular interest to me appear to be weighted the same as a picture of the food a friend is eating at a restaurant that evening. I wish there was a way to prioritize genuine personal stories from friends or the articles they share about arts, sports, technology, and entrepreneurship over some of the other content I see on Facebook. Given that the news-feed algorithm already uses rules to determine which posts to show users and in what order, it would seem logical to provide users with an extension that would enable them to personalize many of those rules to their unique tastes and preferences.

I spoke about this issue with a friend at Facebook, and not surprisingly, I wasn't the first person to have thought about it. In 2015 Facebook began asking people what they wanted out of their news feeds. The answers varied considerably: some wanted to hear more about what friends, family, colleagues, and roommates were up to; others asked for less minutiae—especially information about relationship status changes and profile updates—and instead to be notified when a friend had posted something of substance on his or her wall. In response, Facebook launched a feature that gave people greater control over their news feeds. Using mixer-style controls—the sort that a DJ might use to increase treble and lower bass on a musical track—users could adjust a few sliders to receive, say, more wall post updates and fewer updates about relationship status and profile changes, or vice versa. Users could also choose to learn "More about these friends" or "Less about these friends."

"Maybe one of your friends is dominating your News Feed by always writing boring notes on what she ate yesterday," a Facebook engineer wrote in a blog post about the new tool. Request a tweak to the algorithm via your user preferences page, and "we'll try not to subject you to any more of her culinary ramblings." On the surface, it seemed a friendly move to help customers screen out annoying acquaintances and keep up-to-date with information they genuinely cared about. Below the surface, of course, lay business logic: if users were more likely to engage with the news feed, there was greater potential to pull in advertising dollars.

Unfortunately, when Facebook's engineers examined the usage data after introducing the mixer-style controls, they found that engagement (measured by the number of likes, comments, and clicks on posts, as well as time spent on Facebook) fell. Contrary to expectations, users were interacting less with their news-feed posts than they had before. And surprisingly, although engagement measures fell, people who did customize their news feeds felt more positive about the algorithm.

The decrease in engagement led Facebook to eliminate some of the new features, but also raised many interesting questions. If Facebook's original algorithm was better at predicting the content with which users were likely to engage, why did they resist it in the first place? And why did engagement drop with the new algorithm even as user trust and satisfaction improved?

It could be argued that Facebook's algorithm knows what we want better than we do ourselves. Human psychology drives us to click on the very items that we would like to think we're above; as much as we prefer to believe we have a taste for interesting think pieces, we often succumb to our baser desires (finding out who's dating whom). We could also give the Facebook users who employed these mixer controls some credit: maybe they turned down the volume on roommate relationship status reports because they knew that these were the very sorts of news-feed posts that would tempt them into lingering and clicking; in other words, they *wanted* to engage less with the network, and adjusted the algorithm in a way that would help them do just that.

There is a third possibility, one that moves us beyond the unlikely scenario of companies such as Facebook merely accepting the fact that customers want to engage less with their products. This explanation narrows in on that moment when Facebook users clicked through to their News Feed Preferences page, thought about what they wanted from the app, and took steps to personalize it. It has to do, in other words, with control.

———

Researchers Berkeley Dietvorst, Joe Simmons, and Cade Massey—the same colleagues of mine who showed that we are less likely to trust algorithms once we see them fail—designed an experiment in which subjects were tasked with estimating how well high school students would perform on standardized tests. The study subjects were allowed to use advice from an algorithm (a mathematical model that predicted student scores based on historical patterns) if they wished, and they were allowed to see which factors the algorithm considered when making its own predictions.

The subjects were split into four groups: one group was not allowed to change the estimates provided by the algorithm; two groups could observe the algorithm's estimates and make slight adjustments to the advice it offered; and the last group had free rein to change the algorithm's estimates as much as they wished. Participants were then asked if they wanted to use the algorithm's forecasts. The researchers were seeking to determine if some groups were more likely to adopt the algorithm than others.

They found that users in the first group—those who could not change the algorithm's estimates—were the least likely to adopt it. Those who were given the option to adjust the algorithm's forecasts were significantly more likely to rely on it. In fact, it didn't matter how much control was offered. Merely being allowed to make even tiny tweaks to an algorithm increased the chances that a person would trust it.

"You don't simply present a monolithic model and impose [on users] this is how you should codify your decisions. People will fight that," explains Massey, one of the study's coauthors. Instead, he suggests that algorithms should be introduced, when feasible, as being advisory. "[Users] are a little skeptical early on. Over time, they lean on the model more. Eventually, they are using the entire model as it is even though they have discretion to modify it."

Other research has reached similar conclusions. A group of computer scientists at the University of Minnesota built a recommendation algorithm for a movie website and tested whether users were more satisfied with its outputs if they were given a chance to personalize its inputs (for example, prioritizing new releases). They were.

It seems that those Facebook users who used the mixers to adjust their news-feed algorithms and felt more satisfied with the results were not alone: a little control goes a long way toward improving trust in an algorithm. So it seems logical that such control should be given to them, right? Wrong, said Facebook. While user satisfaction is a good thing, in this instance, it came at the cost of lower engagement. We saw in Chapter One that Match.com's customers often behaved in ways that contradicted their own stated preferences. Similarly, Facebook's users had a poor understanding of their own preferences, which the company's algorithms could infer better from data. So Facebook decided to take back the control it gave users.

Google is likewise denying control to a different set of users for a far more high-minded reason. In 2012 its self-driving car division decided its vehicles were ready for use beyond the test track. Would any of its employees be willing to drive these vehicles on their commutes to work? Many were, and the experiment began, with video cameras recording what went on inside the car and out. The results wound up disturbing the experts—not because of the cars' performance, which was sound, but because of how the humans behaved in them. In spite of the drivers of these vehicles being instructed to remain alert and ready to take the wheel, the Google employees were reclining their seats, zoning out. Chris Urmson, chief technology officer of the division at the time, told an audience at the South by Southwest Conference in Texas: "We had somebody . . . look at their phone and says [*sic*] my battery's low, so turns around, digs in their bag, pulls out their laptop, pulls out their charging cable, plugs the two in, looks up at their phone, yep, charging, and looks back out the window—at sixty-five miles an hour."

There were three ways to react to these findings, recalls Urmson. The company could have ignored this aspect of the test drives and simply continued with them: the self-driving cars themselves had performed well, after all. Or they could have created mechanisms for reminding humans to keep their eyes on the road—a seat that doesn't recline, a mild electric shock if the driver turns around. Or they could have accepted that such responses were inevitable ("human," one might say) and built a better car—one that didn't require human monitoring at all. Google chose the last option, and in November 2015 asked the National Highway Traffic Safety Administration if the company might be allowed to put cars on the road that lacked steering wheels, accelerator pedals, or foot brakes. During the congressional hearing on their proposal, Urmson said "We saw in our own testing that the human drivers can't always be trusted to dip in and out of the task of driving when the car is encouraging them to sit back and relax."

You might ask why Google had to make such an extreme choice. You might also reasonably ask, given the research on how control affects trust, whether so radical a design is even wise, as it could make the difference between the public's embracing self-driving cars and rejecting them. Google's engineers are not unique among designers in believing that end-to-end automation—where algorithms make all the choices, with no guidance from humans—represents the ultimate in product design.

When I started my research on algorithmic decision making, these systems were known as *decision support systems*. The key word here is "support." But algorithms are fast moving from a support role to becoming autonomous decision makers. When robo-advisers invest our money, there is little we need to (or can) do beyond giving them access to our bank accounts. They make all the choices, with little guidance from us—even though research shows that we do, in fact, want some measure of control. By ignoring this issue of trust, engineers may be ensuring that their machines run at optimal performance levels, but they risk the general population's rejecting their innovations outright.

———

Autopilot came early to airplanes. A decade after the Wright brothers first lifted off, a Brooklyn native named Lawrence Sperry persuaded the Navy to test an automated system he had developed, based on a gyroscope, that kept an aircraft level in flight and with its nose pointed in the right direction. The test, which took place in the late summer of 1913 at the tip of one of upstate New York's Finger Lakes, was successful. A year later Sperry wowed crowds at a Paris airshow by having his mechanic climb out on the right wing of his aircraft in flight while holding both his hands high up in the air, demonstrating vividly to the crowd that no one was at the controls. Sperry was awarded $10,000 as a prize.*

———

*Three years later, in November 1916, Sperry crashed his plane after bumping the gyroscope of his plane's autopilot system in the midst of some midflight horizontal tango with a married New York socialite. The pair tumbled, naked, into Long Island's Great South Bay and were fortunately fished out by duck hunters. Sperry insisted that the force of the crash caused them to lose all their clothes. The duck hunters probably had a good laugh, and the media soon credited Sperry with founding the Mile High Club. (Mark Gerchick, "A Brief History of the Mile High Club," *The Atlantic*, January/February 2014, www.theatlantic.com/magazine/archive/2014/01/a-brief-history-of-the-mile-high-club/355733.)

These early experiments (and escapades) all took place on private or military aircraft. An autopilot system got its first use on a commercial airliner in 1931, on a flight between New York and Washington, and autopilot's development quickly turned into a one-way street (though not one without potholes). Today, the technology is used by pilots in many phases of an air journey. Boeing and Airbus have both announced plans for totally self-flying planes—a Google car of the air. But it will be some time before fully autonomous—and pilotless—planes shuttle us around. And that, some critics argue, is the problem.

In the late spring of 2009, an Air France flight from Rio de Janeiro to Paris plummeted into a stormy Atlantic Ocean, killing all 216 passengers and 12 crew members. The cause was human error: as the plane flew into a thunderstorm about three and a half hours into the journey, an airspeed sensor iced over, causing the autopilot to disengage. The pilots were now in charge of keeping the plane in the air. At the same time, and possibly without the pilots realizing it, the fly-by-wire system, which essentially smooths a pilot's maneuvers and guards against potentially catastrophic moves, also disengaged. That meant that when the youngest and least experienced of the three pilots, Pierre-Cédric Bonin, pointed the aircraft's nose upward, driving it higher in the sky, the system didn't—in fact, couldn't—stop him. The engines stalled, and yet Bonin, in a panic, kept directing the aircraft higher. All the system could do was warn the pilots, because they had taken back control. Less than five minutes later—five heartbreaking minutes in the cockpit, according to the transcript of the confused and increasingly terrified conversation among the pilots—the plane hit the water's surface.

It was an unnecessary tragedy, say experts who have examined the evidence. But what would have prevented it? The answer is unclear, because the crash is indirectly rooted in the success of autopilot technology, says William Langewiesche, himself a pilot, who wrote a detailed and harrowing account of the incident for *Vanity Fair*. "Automation has made it more and more unlikely that ordinary airline pilots will ever have to face a raw crisis in flight—but also more and more unlikely that they will be able to cope with such a crisis if one arises," he argues.

Langewiesche's observations suggest that humans will have to be trained better so that they know how to respond during the rare moments when they do need to take over from the autopilot systems. Another solution—Google's approach—would be to never allow autopilot to turn off in the first place. Should Airbus, the aircraft's manufacturer, have removed the steering wheel?

The idea of putting human life entirely in the "hands" of a computer is so anathema to our craving for control that it hardly bears pursuing. And yet, precedent exists. Technologists have pointed to the elevator as a predecessor of the fully automated driverless car. Most of us take automated elevators for granted today, but when elevators were first invented, operators were needed to open and close doors and to use levers or ropes to guide the device to the right floor. According to elevator historian Lee Gray, when "driverless elevators" were first introduced, people hated them. They'd walk into an elevator car and immediately step out, asking "Where's the elevator operator?" But following a strike by operators in New York City in the 1950s, building owners forced the issue. They jettisoned the operators and instead had designers add reassuring features to the machines, most prominent of which was a big red button that said "stop." The button offered no real control to users, who could not, in fact, open doors between floors or override any significant element of the elevator's operating system. If someone did press the button, he was simply directed to use the phone to speak to a remote operator. Still, seeing a stop button gave people a sense of control; they could interrupt the automated system and take over if they needed to do so. The strategy apparently worked, and the usage of automated elevators started increasing. This was consistent with the research from Wharton that showed that trust in algorithms is insensitive to the amount of control offered to the user. As long as users have some control—however minimal—trust is significantly enhanced.

In the driverless Google car, then, that red button would read, "In case of an emergency, press here." (In fact, Google's car really does have a red "e-stop" button, which directs all systems to stop the car as safely and as quickly as possible.)

Both Facebook's and Google's experiences suggest that offering users a significant amount of control can adversely affect the performance of automated systems. At the same time, some degree of user control may be necessary to inspire trust. Current research leads me to believe there is a way to achieve both. This

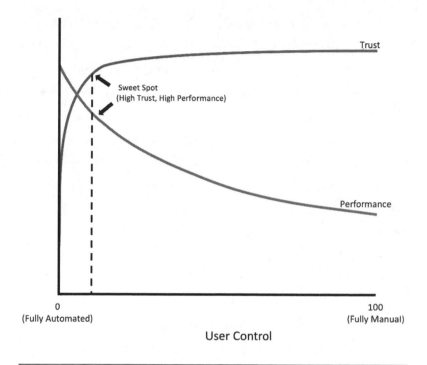

There is a sweet spot of user control at which user trust and algorithm performance are both high enough.

happens at the sweet spot in the figure above—a low level of control at which user trust and system performance are both close to their optimal levels.

It feels somehow wrong to build trust by misrepresenting—to users, to ourselves—who really is in charge. Users are under the illusion of control, but in reality they have limited impact on the decisions being made. Maybe there's another way.

In 2013 researchers from Brazil and France published a paper about the relationship between control and satisfaction—or, in academese, the user's "perceived ability to significantly alter the situation [possibly leading to] stress-reducing and motivation-inducing properties." They asked students in Brazil and France to imagine scenarios in which they purchased products or services; some had the chance to help design these products or services, some did not. Borrowing terminology from psychology, the authors categorized this design input as *behavioral control*, or "the ability to exert a direct influence or action on the environment." In the study, those students given behavioral control rated the purchasing experience as more satisfying than their peers who were denied it. The researchers also had a third and fourth group of students—the former didn't get to control the shape of the product or service, but were given detailed information about the service they were purchasing (which the researchers called *cognitive control*), while the latter didn't get to control the shape of the product or service, but were told they could get their money back if they were not happy (*decisional control*). Both groups were more satisfied with the experience than the control group not offered these perks.

And so emerges a framework where product designers can build trust in their algorithms without endangering their customers (or balance sheets). The highest level of control a user interface designer can offer users is behavioral control. While it's hard to give users complete control over the data, the model, or the inference of an algorithm without compromising its performance, it is possible to provide selective behavioral control. For example, on Netflix and Pandora, users can respond with "thumbs up" or "thumbs down" feedback to recommendations, which in turn will be used by the algorithm to improve future recommendations. Similarly, after its fake news debacle, Facebook made it easy to report hate speech, false reporting, unauthorized selling, and nudity in posts that appear in news feeds. It allows Facebook's algorithm to learn from the feedback and correct itself when it fails to recognize offensive or untrue material. This is genuine behavioral control that affects what kinds of content the news-feed algorithm allows through. Of course, anyone can try to use this feedback loop to his own ends: if an uninformed or malicious individual tags a post as false news and urges friends to do the same, the algorithm might be fooled into hiding it. In such a scenario, providing unmonitored user control can backfire. Still, whether used for good ends or ill, the user has some control over the choices made by the algorithm, if not the ability to rewrite the algorithm itself.

Where behavioral control is risky, decisional control can enhance trust without undermining algorithm performance. Google's search algorithm offers decisional control by returning a long list of hits for every search query and allowing the user to select the one that best fits her needs. Even if the first one or two results are not accurate, there are other options further down the list, or even through pages and pages of results, to choose a better match.

Decisional control is relevant elsewhere, too. As Ranjani Ramamurthy, the physician working at Microsoft, observes: "Doctors want to be the final decision makers. So let the doctors hold the steering wheel. Like when Gmail suggests smart replies, and you choose from them, AI systems can give doctors options and reasoning and then they can choose. They will be more willing to adopt it." And they'll need to adopt it, she adds, because healthcare is changing in ways that will only put further demands on doctors' time. Without intelligent algorithms, there will be no way to meet these burdens.

And then there is cognitive control, meaning awareness of what, exactly, the algorithm is doing. I find it slightly misleading to even call this control and prefer to describe it as transparency. But that doesn't mean that I think it is any less important. In fact, transparency is getting a lot of buzz among AI researchers and social scientists. Let's see why transparency has become the talk of the AI town.

9.

Inside the Black Box

An algorithm must be seen to be believed.

Donald Knuth, computer scientist

Every step toward inscrutability is a step away from accountability. . . . Unknowability might be an unavoidable consequence of self-aware, self-improving software.

James Barrat, *Our Final Invention: Artificial Intelligence and the End of the Human Era*

One fine summer morning, you show up for a scheduled appointment for your regular checkup at the highly rated local health clinic. You walk in feeling fine. You raise your arm and say, "Doc, it hurts when I do this." The doctor responds, "Then don't do that." You both chuckle. But several tests later, your mood changes. Your internist, friendly old Dr. Culverton Smith, has some bad news.

"I'm afraid you're at high risk for Tapanuli fever," Dr. Smith says. "It's inevitably fatal. The good news is that there's a medication that can help prevent it. I recommend you start taking it immediately. It may make you light-headed, irritable, and occasionally nauseous. But that's a small price to pay to avoid the fever."

You are taken aback. "I've never heard of this disease," you protest as he scribbles out a prescription. "How do you know I'm at risk for it?"

Dr. Smith shows you a computer printout filled with incomprehensible numbers and terms. But he points to a line near the bottom of the form that reads: "TAPANULI FEVER: 17.88." "That risk factor's way too high," he explains. "We want to get it down below five. The pills should help."

"But where did that number come from?" you ask.

Dr. Smith shrugs. "It's our new AI system. It's all the rage these days. The software has the knowledge of a thousand top diagnosticians built into it. Not much point in questioning what it has to say—not if you want to stay alive, that is."

You take the prescription and leave. But on the drive home, you can't decide whether to stop at the pharmacy. You believe in technology and the marvels of machine learning. But do you really want to put up with light-headedness, irritability, and nausea to fend off the possibility of some unknown disease even if Dr. Smith's computer software says you should? When it comes right down to it, do you trust the algorithm?

If your answer is no, you might want to reflect on the reasons why.

A big part of the problem may be the vagueness of the doctor's explanation. What if, in answer to your question, "Where did that number come from?" he had replied, "Your blood test this afternoon shows you have unusually low levels of three proteins that help bolster your immune defenses against Tapanuli fever. And the genome analysis we did last fall had already indicated a heightened vulnerability to several syndromes associated with Southeast Asian ancestry. A study from the *New Jersey Journal of Medicine* found that this combination of traits leads to a 94 percent increase in incidence of Tapanuli fever. The software puts all this data together and calculates your risk factor—the number I showed you on your printout." Hearing those details, you'd probably find the case for medication more compelling even if you didn't really understand everything the doctor said.

Of course, the above story is fabricated one, and Tapanuli fever is a fictitious disease.* But because software employing AI

---

*Tapanuli fever appears in "The Adventure of the Dying Detective," a Sherlock Holmes short story written in 1913 by Sir Arthur Conan Doyle. In the story, Mr. Culverton Smith, a plantation owner from Sumatra, cultures a bacterium and infects his nephew with the mysterious disease. Sherlock Holmes solves the mystery. Scientists who compared the symptoms of Tapanuli fever with those of known infectious diseases from Southeast Asia believe that Conan Doyle may have gotten the inspiration for Tapanuli fever from melioidosis, an infectious disease first reported from Burma (now Myanmar) in 1912. Today, AI systems can probably do a better job of matching a disease's symptoms with past case records. Further, not far from Holmes's residence on Baker Street in London, UK police are experimenting with an AI-based detective system. Once a case arrives, the system scans through millions of police records to identify other incidents that could be related based on the time, location, or manner of the crime. Perhaps Sherlock Holmes would have

is now being used to diagnose illnesses and calculate risk factors for various conditions, the question of what it takes for patients—and physicians, too—to trust an algorithm regarding matters of sickness and health is a real one. And it is transparency, research suggests, that is the key to understanding, acceptance, and belief. Let people look inside the black box of the algorithm, the thinking goes, and their mistrust, hostility, and fear will gradually melt away.

That argument sounds logical enough. But is it true? Is transparency the major factor in fostering trust in algorithms? As with so much in this area, the answer is interesting . . . and complicated.

———

Clifford Nass had a problem. Students in his popular Stanford University class on technology interface design were complaining about their grades on the midterm exam. While such complaints are all too common for professors, the complaints had a specific, substantive basis in this case. Students in one section of the course had discovered that they were receiving significantly

———

been written very differently in the age of AI. (Setu K. Vora, MD, "Sherlock Holmes and a Biological Weapon," *JRSM* 95, no. 2 [February 2002]: 101–3, www .ncbi.nlm.nih.gov/pmc/articles/PMC1279324; Timothy Revell, "AI Detective Analyses Police Data to Learn How to Crack Cases," *New Scientist*, May 10, 2017, www.newscientist.com/article/mg23431254–000-ai-detective-analyses-police -data-to-learn-how-to-crack-cases.)

lower exam grades than their counterparts in another section even when their essay responses were similar.

The cause of the problem wasn't hard to identify. Two different teaching assistants had graded the papers. Since the scoring of essay responses is inherently subjective, it's not surprising that TAs differ in their grading. One way to minimize this problem is to assign specific TAs to grade specific test questions for the entire group of students. In this system, any two students comparing their grades for a given question can feel that grading is fair because the same TA read both the answers. But Nass had chosen not to follow this procedure. Because there were more than two hundred students in the class, but only two questions on the midterm, Nass had divided the grading among TAs by class section. This simple, efficient decision introduced a fatal element of bias, and unleashed justifiable dissent from his students.

Nass could simply have backed down, apologized, and adopted the divide-by-question system for future exams. But as a leading expert on human-computer interactions, he instead saw an opportunity for a statistical solution. Using an idea suggested by one of his TAs, Nass decided to fix the grading bias by creating an algorithm.

Nass and a research assistant worked together to measure the grading tendencies of each TA based on his or her scoring of similar problem sets. They then created a simple statistical model to adjust student scores to counteract the individual scoring biases—for example, by raising grades by five percent on papers scored by a TA known to give grades five percent lower than average.

Nass was confident that his students would be pleased. He sent them emails containing both their original grades and adjusted grades based on his simple algorithm. In the spirit of openness, he also carefully explained the details of his adjustment algorithm and how it ensured the greatest possible fairness.

Nass was startled when the students responded with further complaints—some even angrier than the initial ones.

Something had clearly gone wrong.

At the heart of this conundrum are the tangled vines of transparency and trust. When we interact with algorithms, we know we are dealing with machines. Yet somehow their intelligence and their ability to mimic our own patterns of thought and communication confuse us into viewing them as human. Researchers have observed that when computer users are asked to describe how machines interact with them, they use anthropomorphic terms such as "integrity," "honesty," and "cruelty." I have done the same in this book whenever I have referred to algorithms' "behavior" or their "going rogue." Our language, at least, would suggest that we expect the same degree of trustworthiness, benevolence, and fairness from the computer algorithms we deal with as we do from our human peers.

This helps to explain why harnessing the power of transparency to induce greater trust in algorithms is more difficult than one might assume. The complications with transparency in general, and Nass's unsuccessful foray into grading transparency in particular, can be seen in *massive open online courses*, better known as MOOCs. Unconstrained by factors such as student location or classroom size, universities, colleges, and educational platforms such as Coursera offer online classes that can be taken by tens of thousands of students. For example, the entrepreneurship courses that I have taught on Coursera have been taken by nearly 100,000 students (as compared to roughly 2,500 students over the course of fifteen years in brick-and-mortar university classrooms). The reach of MOOCs is great, but they have their own challenges—for example, how to actively engage the many students with whom you don't interact, or how to grade complex assignments such as essays or designs turned in by a class numbering more than ten thousand. Most MOOCs utilize peer grading rather than having TAs score student papers: in other words, the students are asked to evaluate one another's work. The notion might sound odd at first, but studies have shown that peer grading is actually comparable to grading by an instructor. Anonymous peer grading bolsters the accuracy of the scores by reducing favoritism and other such concerns as well as eliminating the need to hire hundreds of graders for each course. However, it does not do away with the problem of grader bias—in fact, it intensifies it, because it involves many more graders with varying personalities and tendencies.

René Kizilcec, a young Stanford PhD student, wanted to

solve this grader bias issue. His interest was not accidental. Nass was in fact his adviser, and he had watched the turmoil unfold in the class. When he enrolled as Nass's PhD student, Kizilcec had planned to work on the development of trust-inducing interfaces for semi-autonomous vehicles. But in November 2013, tragedy struck when the fifty-five-year-old Nass suffered a heart attack and died. Left without his admired adviser, Kizilcec found himself thinking more and more about the grading problem that Nass had left unsolved.

Kizilcec found that many of the MOOCs were using variants of a grade adjustment algorithm created by one of Kizilcec's colleagues. Interestingly, none of the MOOCs explained this grading policy to their students. The MOOC managers were unsure of the wisdom of communicating to students how their grades were determined, and, even if they did, how to do so effectively. For the students, the stakes were high, because the grades determined whether or not they received a certificate for completing the course.

Kizilcec set out to create an online version of Nass's original experiment with algorithmically adjusted grades—and to use it to test how transparency could ultimately change the degree of trust that students would have in the algorithms that affected them. He began with a group of 103 students who had submitted essays to be peer graded. Each essay was graded by multiple peers. Kizilcec asked these students to state the grade they expected to receive. Next, each student received both a *combined grade*—a simple average of the grades assigned by a group of peer graders—and a *computed grade*, one adjusted by an algorithm that accounted for each grader's bias.

To test the effect of transparency upon trust, Kizilcec varied the amount of information each student received about the grading process. One set of students was provided minimal transparency about the workings of the algorithm and was simply informed of the computed grade.

A second subset of students was given an entire paragraph explaining how the grades were adjusted by a simple algorithm: "Your computed grade is X, which is based on the grades you received from your peers and adjusted for their bias and accuracy in grading. The accuracy and bias are estimated using a statistical procedure that employs an expectation maximization algorithm with a prior for class grades. This adjusts your grade for easy/harsh graders and grader proficiency."

Immediately after receiving this information, participants were asked several questions to assess their trust in the peer grading system. The questions dealt with comprehension of the process ("To what extent do you understand how your grade is computed in peer grading?") as well as perceived fairness, accuracy, and finally, trust.

Based on their original anticipated grades and their final grades, Kizilcec sorted the students into two groups: those who had received a grade similar to expectations, and those who had suffered an *expectation violation*—that is, they received a lower grade than they had anticipated. The attitudes of the two groups toward grading transparency proved to be dramatically different.

For students whose grade expectations had been met or exceeded, the level of transparency did not affect their levels of trust. But for those who had received an unpleasant surprise, the level of trust was strongly linked to the transparency level. The disappointed students who had been given more information about the grading procedure—the second, greater transparency condition—rated their trust in the grading system higher than those who had received the bare-bones explanation.

Kizilcec explained this result by referring to a human tendency to apply greater scrutiny to information when expectations are violated, and the idea that people are often satisfied with a system, even when faced with a negative or disappointing result, as long as they believe that the underlying process is fair. A grading algorithm is an attempt to adjust for biases and inaccuracies. "We agree that is the right thing to do even if the outcome might be negative for us . . . even if [our] grade is adjusted down," says Kizilcec. That meant that even students who received poor grades were willing to trust the system if the information they got about the process assured them that every effort had been made to ensure that the grades were fair.

Where, then, had Nass gone wrong? Why didn't his in-depth explanation of the grading algorithm win students' trust and quell their complaints?

The answer is provided by another aspect of Kizilcec's experiment. In fact, Kizilcec tested not two tiers of transparency but three. The two levels mentioned above were labeled low and medium. A third set of students received not only the paragraph of explanation from the medium level, but also their individual raw peer-graded scores, along with details on how exactly these raw scores were combined and adjusted to arrive at the final grade. This was labeled high transparency.

And here is where the experimental results contained a surprise. Among students with violated expectations, the medium transparency level increased trust relative to the low level. But those who experienced the high transparency level did not, as you might expect, experience an even greater sense of trust in the algorithm. Instead, they reported even *less* trust than those in the low transparency group!

What did this all mean?

The results stem, Kizilcec argues, from our tendency to anthropomorphize machines, and from the social rules and heuristics we employ in human interactions. When we meet new people, we are hesitant to develop close ties of trust and friendship with them until we see some evidence that they are honest and forthright. We expect a degree of transparency from others, and distrust those who withhold, so we tend to avoid people who conceal their thoughts and intentions. Kizilcec points out that many of us also find it difficult to like and trust people who are excessively transparent. Those who spend too much time explaining and justifying their intentions often arouse our suspicions, to the point that we start to wonder, "What is he trying to prove?"

For human beings, then, there is such a thing as the "right" amount of transparency—not too little, not too much. Kizilcec argues that the same applies to algorithms. Too much information can undermine user trust as much as too little. Kizilcec believes—and has peer-reviewed reason to believe—that there is a similar sweet spot for trust in human-algorithm interactions.

We now have a basis to understand where Clifford Nass went wrong. Nass informed his students how their newly adjusted grades had been computed, his goal being to gain their trust through algorithmic transparency. But Nass actually *over-explained* the algorithm. In two lengthy emails, he detailed the precise methods used to calculate the grades. In one instance, he wrote: "With those data in hand, we can now compute your Midterm Q1 adjusted. The formula is: Midterm Q1 Adjusted = ((Midterm Q1 number wrong—Median FOR YOUR GRADER)/ (.5*interquartile range FOR YOUR GRADER))+4." This explanation was followed by even more specific calculations using hypothetical graders and scores.

Nass would probably have won over his students if he'd provided them with just enough information to convince them that the grade adjustment procedure was fair—and stopped there. By offering such a highly detailed explanation, he triggered a trust backlash. Perhaps the bewildering level of detail they were given inadvertently shifted the students' focus from the fairness of the process back to their unfavorable grades or to their lack of understanding of the actual procedure, thereby undoing whatever gains in trust he had hoped to achieve.

To use the modern expression, it was a case of TMI—too much information.

———

You are planning to buy an Android phone with superior camera features but are confused by the sheer number of options available: Samsung, LG, Google Pixel, HTC, and many other brands. You visit a store and ask a sales rep for some recommendations. He asks you a series of questions and then recommends a model by Samsung that costs $450. You wonder whether the rep is trying to trick you into buying one of the more expensive models. She notices your hesitation and explains her recommendation.

Which of these explanations is most likely to allay your distrust of the commission-earning rep?

1. "Based on your answers, I considered the storage capacity, CPU power, camera, screen size, screen resolution, weight, and battery capacity you'll need. Next, I found the lowest priced phone that fits these needs."
2. "I recommended this model because you will be taking lots of photos for your work on it and you will need a camera with good optical zoom and low-light performance. You will need at least 32 GB storage. This is the best phone with that spec."
3. "It's hard to get a phone with all the features while keeping the cost less than $400. Based on your needs, I

———

decided to prioritize the camera and storage space. To reduce the cost, I chose a phone with a smaller screen size and lower screen resolution. But this still means it costs $450."

Each message offers a different type of transparency, and each might evoke very different feelings.

Research on decision support systems would label these as *how*, *why*, and *trade-off* explanations. The first describes the rep's line of reasoning and some details of how she arrived at her suggestion. The second provides justifications for the suggestion, or the purpose behind it ("you will be taking lots of photos for your work on it"). And the third reveals the ways in which the rep is seeking to balance various criteria in formulating the recommendation (the desire for advanced features versus cost of the phone).

Research aimed at defining precisely how transparency can best enhance trust is still in its infancy. But according to a study by Weiquan Wang and Izak Benbasat at the University of British Columbia, in order to understand how the type of explanation matters, you need to first consider the nature of the trust deficit.

Wang and Benbasat consider the sort of recommendation algorithm we talked about in Chapter Three. Specifically, instead of a sales rep, they evaluate an algorithm designed to help people choose products to buy. A *how* explanation will assure the customer that the algorithm knows its stuff. This alleviates what academics call *weakened competence belief*, and it's certainly valuable when we shop for a specialized electronic or mechanical device—a car, a computer, an advanced music system, or a phone. We may find it difficult to determine whether a particular algorithm truly has expertise in such gadgets or is simply throwing around impressive-sounding terms. The result is that we may doubt whether it is genuinely competent at its job.

The recommendation algorithm might instead decide to tackle a different type of trust deficit: the customer suspecting its motives. They might wonder if it's looking to maximize its commissions rather than find the best camera phone for them (*weakened benevolence belief*, in academic terms). A *why* explanation will try to alleviate such doubts. As Kizilcec says, "One way we trust someone is that we know they are experts in their domain. They know the facts and the science in that area. That can be established by an AI system by sharing its track record. But there's another part to this. We only trust someone when we know they are on our side, or at least the side we think is the right side."

Then there's a third obstacle: *weakened integrity belief*. Will an algorithm uphold commonly held values such as honesty, fairness, and promise keeping?

In order to test whether specific types of transparency could help to overcome these obstacles, the researchers designed a recommendation engine and asked study participants to use it to choose a camera for a close friend and another for a family member. Participants were divided randomly into three groups. One group was given a version of the algorithm that offered *how* explanations for its choices, another group got *why* explanations, and a third group got *trade-off* explanations. Afterward, the participants were asked to write a justification for their product choices. They then completed a questionnaire designed to assess their trust in the algorithm.

The researchers found that *how* explanations significantly increased users' competence belief—that is, their readiness to believe that the algorithm did in fact have the skill and knowledge it claimed. *How* explanations had a small positive impact on users' benevolence belief—their acceptance of the algorithm's commitment to operating on their behalf rather than in the best interests of some other party. But *how* explanations did little to boost users' trust in the machine's integrity. Meanwhile, *why* explanations significantly increased users' benevolence belief but had little impact on their belief in the system's expertise or integrity. And *trade-off* explanations significantly increased their integrity belief but barely nudged their belief in the algorithm's expertise or benevolence.

The implication is that interface designers dealing with a problem of user mistrust would be well advised to identify precisely what kind of mistrust is most prevalent in a given situation—and to design the explanations they provide to match the specific problem.

When Nass drafted his emails to students explaining his algorithm, he probably wasn't thinking about the category of explanation he was providing. He offered all three types of transparency in his emails, but if he had been able to determine whether students doubted the competence, benevolence, or integrity of the algorithm, he could have tailored his explanation accordingly and not burdened them with too much information.

Perhaps I am guilty of doing the same here. Before I lose your trust, let me summarize. Much more study and experimentation is needed before we can state definitively that a robust, tested protocol for algorithmic transparency has been developed. But these early efforts appear to demonstrate that the link between transparency and trust is far from a simple one. Software engineers, interface designers, and other parties interested in enhancing user trust can't expect to meet the challenge simply by throwing an explanation of their algorithm up on the computer screen and checking off "transparency" on their to-do lists. Instead, any explanation has to be carefully designed and calibrated to address the particular trust issues bedeviling that specific user-algorithm relationship.

There's another benefit to carefully calibrated transparency: The process of making algorithmic decisions more transparent forces programmers to think harder about the rationale behind those decisions. Will this help prevent the unanticipated consequences we discussed in Part One of this book? While it can't hurt, there's a danger in treating transparency as a potential immunization against rogue algorithms. Some researchers argue that transparency without the power to change the underlying biased data or logic is nothing but an illusion. That said, transparency does more than enhance trust. It can be seen as a means through which we can increase accountability and diagnose problematic decisions.

To see that, we should distinguish between a layperson using an algorithm and a more technical person who is auditing it and the role that transparency plays for both sides. "Both sides are important. If we get only one right, it won't work," says Kizilcec, whose research on how explanations shape user attitudes emphasizes the user side. But Kizilcec acknowledges that the stakes are a lot higher than just technology acceptance. To manage many of the unanticipated consequences of algorithmic decisions, we also need to think about how transparency aids the auditing of algorithms. And while a very high level of transparency has the potential to reduce user trust, it is critical for the technical individual auditing the system.

But how do we achieve a high enough level of transparency so that regulators can effectively audit algorithms?

One obvious solution for making algorithms more transparent would call for simply allowing the source code of the algorithm—the actual text of the underlying software—to be made public. This is often called *technical transparency*. And while it might sound like the ultimate in transparency, in reality it is not that simple.

In August 2017 James Vacca, a New York City Council member, introduced a bill related to the use of automated decision systems by the city's agencies. The bill stemmed from Vacca's frustrations at the city's inability to explain how police officers were assigned to different precincts. He soon learned that algorithms not only made these choices, but were also responsible for a number of other important municipal decisions, such as the matching of students to public schools and assessing teacher performance. The original draft of Vacca's bill was met with resistance. According to reports, the primary stumbling block was the proposed legislation's requirement that whenever a city agency planned to use an automated system to allocate resources or services, the source code of the system would have to be made public.

In a world where most of the algorithms being deployed are created and managed by for-profit companies, technical transparency generates serious legal and economic problems. Many businesses regard their algorithms as highly valuable forms of intellectual property that they are loath to reveal publicly, lest competitors copy them. For this reason, some attempts to impose transparency requirements on software firms have provided that source code be revealed to regulators or auditors only in the event of a serious problem. (We saw an example of this in the case of the 2012 "flash crash" on Wall Street, when regulators with the Commodity Futures Trading Commission demanded access to the source code of the algorithms that had caused a temporary loss of up to a trillion dollars in stock market value.) If humans are charged with evaluating an algorithm's source code, the value of transparency will depend on the expertise and the credibility of the regulators and auditors who study the algorithm and vouch for its integrity. In effect, this approach merely shifts the burden of belief from the algorithm itself to the experts who evaluate and approve it. I am not hopeful about this particular path.

Another problem with technical transparency is that revealing all aspects of a system makes it vulnerable to gaming. Suppose, for example, that I release to all my students the complete source code for an algorithm I have developed for grading the essays on their final exams. It is easy to imagine one of them—call her Jane—studying the code and noticing a loophole of which I was unaware. Maybe, for example, the algorithm seeks evidence that the students have done research by looking for words such as "According to published accounts." Jane then deliberately uses this phrase at the start of every paragraph in her essays—and receives the highest grade in the class as a result.

Malevolent actors can manipulate transparent systems to create more-serious negative impacts. For example, knowledge of Google's source code could enable internet companies to trick the search engine into ranking their websites higher, even if their site's content is irrelevant to a user's search query. Public dissemination of the source code used by electronic voting systems might increase public confidence in the sanctity of the ballot but it would also provide plenty of extra ammunition to use in undermining the integrity of election results.

The New York City Council eventually passed a tamer version of Vacca's bill, which merely required setting up a fact-finding task force to study the matter further and come up with recommendations.

While technical transparency raises legitimate economic and legal concerns, the most important challenge is that the very nature of modern AI makes technical transparency increasingly irrelevant in explaining the behavior of algorithms. As we have seen, modern algorithms develop significant portions of their logic through machine learning. Some of today's most complex systems have only a few hundred lines of code, and reading them may reveal very little about why the algorithm makes the choices it does.

I believe the better approach is the one that Clifford Nass had tried: providing detailed explanations of the how, the why, and the trade-offs behind algorithmic decisions. How do we accomplish this in light of the predictability-resilience paradox? The reasoning behind a deep learning algorithm's decisions is often impenetrable to even the programmer who created it. In a world of opaque algorithms, how can we know why an algorithm decided not to approve my loan application when it approved my neighbor's?

———

Researchers at the University of Washington have developed an approach to help interpret individual decisions of machine learning systems. Their approach highlights the relative importance of different factors driving any individual decision. For example, if a model assigns a student a grade of 73, the proposed approach evaluates how the predicted grade changes with minor modifications in the main inputs (what happens if word count is reduced by 10 percent or if the essay cited fewer research papers). Similarly, researchers at Carnegie Mellon University have developed a system for increasing the transparency of algorithms and uncovering any hidden biases they might contain. The system works by analyzing various inputs used by a decision-making algorithm, measuring the impact of each of the inputs individually and in groups, and finally reporting the set of inputs that had the largest impact on the final decision. When applied to an essay-grading algorithm, it might analyze how changes in inputs such as word count affected the final grade and provide an explanation such as: "Tim received a score of 73 on his exam. Of Tim's score, 49 percent is explained by content matches with key concepts listed in the grading key; 18 percent is explained by the fact that Tim's essay exceeded the word-count threshold of 1,000 words; 13 percent is explained by the fact that Tim's essay mentioned relevant source documents in appropriate contexts. The rest of Tim's score is explained by several other less-significant factors." This kind of analysis would help the designer modify the program, if necessary, as well as provide end users with answers to *how* questions and thereby bolster some types of trust in the system.

Another approach comes from researchers at the University of California, Berkeley, and the Max Planck Institute for Informatics who have been developing image recognition algorithms that can explain their own activities. After the algorithm analyzes a picture, it not only attempts to identify the image, but also provides a textual explanation. For instance, if the algorithm recognizes a picture as depicting a game of baseball, it would clarify that this decision was based on its observing a player holding or swinging a bat. The justification provided by the algorithm essentially offers a human interpretation for its actions.

Unfortunately, there exist a number of barriers to making modern algorithms fully transparent. One such arises from the fact that some algorithms are deliberately designed to include an element of randomness. This randomness—"noise" injected into the data—serves as a source of fairness in the system. Consider, for example, an algorithm used by a bank to make decisions on granting loans to applicants. If members of minority groups tend to have their loan applications declined because of a bias in an algorithm, including a random factor in the process can ensure that some small number will get the loans anyway. The system can then observe the default rate among these individuals and correct its bias. Randomness also allows these systems to try new decisions and not get caught up in a loop wherein biased data lead to biased machine learning algorithms that perpetuate the biased decision making. While random noise in the decision process has some merit, it would be difficult to make the following explanation satisfactory to a consumer: "Even though you and your neighbor have equally good loan applications, your neighbor got the loan and you got turned down because of random noise we inject into our approval process to improve fairness."

In 2016, the Defense Advanced Research Projects Agency (DARPA), a branch of the U.S. Department of Defense that develops emerging technologies for military use, announced a new research program on XAI, which stands for Explainable Artificial Intelligence. This four-year project brings together academic and industry experts to create algorithms and models that can explain their results. The hope is that creating a new process of machine learning that is conducive to an explanation-based model and interface will increase our understanding of algorithmic behaviors—including their failures and the steps required to correct them.

A solution to the interconnected problems of transparency and trust could bring us closer to the day when people in all kinds of situations—not just students submitting essays to be graded or shoppers seeking advice about a product, but also passengers in driverless cars, litigants in a court of law, and even patients seeking a diagnosis—will be willing and even happy to accept the guidance of an unseen and somewhat unknown algorithmic presence.

10.

An Algorithmic Bill of Rights

Crying is all right in its way while it lasts. But you have to stop sooner or later, and then you still have to decide what to do.

C. S. Lewis, *The Silver Chair*

The Three Laws of Robotics:

1: A robot may not injure a human being or, through inaction, allow a human being to come to harm;

2: A robot must obey the orders given it by human beings except where such orders would conflict with the First Law;

3: A robot must protect its own existence as long as such protection does not conflict with the First or Second Law;

The Zeroth Law: A robot may not harm humanity, or, by inaction, allow humanity to come to harm.

Isaac Asimov, *I, Robot*

One Tuesday morning a few months ago, I visited the National Constitution Center in downtown Philadelphia, which proudly bills itself as America's most hands-on history museum. The museum is just four blocks from my home, and whenever I walk past it I make a mental note that I ought to drop in more often—but my recent visit was my first in a decade.

I walked up the stairs and made my way into the first exhibit space. At first glance it appeared crowded, but then I realized that almost all of the figures surrounding me were life-size statues. On most weekends the center is packed with tourists, but that weekday morning, the first room, known as Signers' Hall, contained just me, a group of four schoolkids, and five guides in red T-shirts, standing around. I was amused that there were as many guides as visitors in the room that day.

In less than a minute, one of the guides approached me. A friendly woman apparently in her mid-seventies—perhaps a retiree who volunteered at the museum—introduced herself as Joyce and asked, "Do you have any questions?"

I felt it would be polite to come up with something. "Why does this room have so many statues?" I asked. It wasn't exactly the most intelligent question, but it was the best I could come up with on the fly. To my surprise, Joyce was delighted. "Signers' Hall depicts the final day of the Constitutional Convention of 1787," she explained. "The forty-two bronze statues represent the founders who took part in the debates about our national system of government. Their arrangement is based on a contemporary painting, and each of the statues is correct in terms of body shape and height."

"Really?" I muttered.

Joyce nodded proudly. "Their dimensions are based on tailors' measurements of their clothes. Look closely and you may recognize some of their faces. That's George Washington over there. This is Ben Franklin, of course. And here's Alexander Hamilton—the current star of the exhibit thanks to the Broadway musical."

I found my attention drawn to a group of three statues that seemed oddly placed at some distance from the other figures. "Why are these over here?" I asked.

"Oh, these are the dissenters," Joyce explained. "These men refused to sign the new constitution." She motioned a colleague over. "Bob can tell you more about the dissenters."

Bob, another guide in his seventies, was also excited to have a visitor on a slow day. "We have statues of three dissenters," Bob told me. "George Mason and Edmund Randolph of Virginia, and Elbridge Gerry of Massachusetts. They worried that the new national government might become a new form of tyranny, not so different from the one that they had recently overthrown. So they demanded some kind of guarantee that the rights of the people would not be forgotten. Those demands led to the Bill of Rights—the first ten amendments to the Constitution. Those amendments list specific rights that the government must not violate, ranging from freedom of religion and the right to assembly to the guarantee of a trial by jury."

I nodded. This was all interesting, but I had been hoping to do some of the tour alone. I thought of ways to excuse myself, but it was becoming clear that the guides were not going to let me be. Not on a day with so few visitors.

As I debated my best course of action, Bob continued his explanation. "The purpose of the Constitution was to establish the kind of strong central government that our nation needed," he said. "But the dissenters worried that we were replacing King George III with King George Washington. They feared that the new federal government might become too powerful."

"Well, today the power is with the big corporations," I said, as a way of making polite conversation.

"Maybe we need a new Bill of Rights to deal with that!" Bob replied with a laugh.

I smiled in response. But as I thought about what he had observed, I turned to him and said, "You are right. A bill of rights is what we need after all." I proceeded to describe the book I was working on and the challenges with new technologies. Bob was pleased to finally have my attention. "Let me show you the Bill of Rights. It might inspire you," he said as he led me to another room.

———

The Bill of Rights represented the first time that any national constitution explicitly included protections for the rights of citizens. But it did not emerge from a vacuum. Bob explained that it drew inspiration from a host of earlier documents, including the Magna Carta, the charter of rights signed by the English King John in 1215; the English Bill of Rights of 1689; and the Virginia Declaration of Rights. The U.S. Bill of Rights was a richer, stronger product because it was built on earlier efforts.

Today, in an era when corporations are rapidly rolling out advanced artificial intelligence and machine learning, it makes sense for us to be thinking about an algorithmic bill of rights that will protect society. The question is whether there are meaningful earlier efforts on which we can build. Fortunately, many organizations and individuals are thinking and debating the nature of the challenges we face in the age of powerful algorithms—along with potential solutions. We're in a position to use some of their most useful ideas as we consider how to develop and deploy new algorithmic tools.

In October 2016, the White House Office of Science and Technology Policy (OSTP) released a report titled *Preparing for the Future of Artificial Intelligence*. The document explores applications of AI for the public good as well as the challenges it presents, including implications for the workforce and notions of fairness, safety, and governance, and concludes with a series of twenty-three recommendations. Understandably, most are aimed at providing government agencies with guidelines on their use of AI. And many—as one might expect from a document that represents the current consensus among a large group of diverse experts—are a bit vague and somewhat anodyne. Here are two examples:

Recommendation 5: Agencies should draw on appropriate technical expertise at the senior level when setting regulatory policy for AI-enabled products.

Recommendation 16: Federal agencies that use AI-based systems to make or provide decision support for consequential decisions about individuals should take extra care to ensure the efficacy and fairness of those systems, based on evidence-based verification and validation.

Other efforts have gone beyond simply presenting the problems and have attempted to craft solutions that can actually be implemented. In January 2017, the US Public Policy Council of the Association for Computing Machinery (ACM), which consists of educators, researchers, and professionals in the world of information technology, outlined a set of guiding principles that could serve as a precursor for an algorithmic bill of rights. These principles cover seven general areas:

1. **Awareness**—those who design, implement, and use algorithms must be aware of their potential biases and possible harm, and take these into account in their practices.
2. **Access and redress**—those who are negatively affected by algorithms must have systems that enable them to question the decisions and seek redress.
3. **Accountability**—organizations that use algorithms must

take responsibility for the decisions those algorithms reach, even if it is not feasible to explain how the algorithms arrive at those decisions.

4. **Explanation**—those affected by algorithms should be given explanations of the decisions and the procedures that generated them.

5. **Data provenance**—those who design and use algorithms should maintain records on the data used to train the algorithms and make those records available to appropriate individuals to be studied for possible biases.

6. **Auditability**—algorithms and data should be recorded so that they can be audited in cases of possible harm.

7. **Validation and testing**—organizations that use algorithms should test them regularly for bias and make the results publicly available.

The AI Now Institute at New York University, an interdisciplinary research center dedicated to understanding the social implications of artificial intelligence, also issued a list of recommendations in 2017 for those working in the field. Some of their recommendations overlap with ACM's principles. But they also cover new ground, such as the following:

> Core public agencies, such as those responsible for criminal justice, healthcare, welfare, and education (e.g. "high-stakes" domains), should no longer use "black box" AI and algorithmic systems. This includes the unreviewed or

unvalidated use of pre-trained models, AI systems licensed from third party vendors, and algorithmic processes created in-house. The use of such systems by public agencies raises serious due process concerns, and at a minimum they should be available for public auditing, testing, and review, and subject to accountability standards.

These various sets of recommendations and guiding principles are important elements in a widening, intensifying conversation about algorithmic decision making and its challenges. But of course they differ from a true bill of rights in one crucial way: no one is empowered to actually *enforce* them. So it's not surprising that voices are now emerging that want to take principles like those proposed by the ACM and give them teeth by creating regulatory bodies with enforcement power.

One proponent is Ben Shneiderman, a professor of computer science at the University of Maryland, whose research helped pave the way to such breakthroughs as the touch screen used on smartphones. In his May 2017 Turing Lecture at the British Library in London, Shneiderman issued a call for a National Algorithmic Safety Board. Modeled on the Federal Reserve Board, it would be staffed by experts who rotate in and out of their positions regularly and are given the power to audit algorithmic processes, subpoena critical information, and issue rulings that industry participants would be required to obey.

In December 2017, New York City passed a law to set up a

new Automated Decision Systems Task Force to monitor the algorithms used by municipal agencies. The establishment of a task force is a good first step and will likely have an impact on other cities and states around the world. The government of Singapore has set up a similar advisory council on the ethical use of AI. It has so far chosen to regulate lightly, and instead work with the industry to develop advisory guidelines and best practices for companies to adopt voluntarily.

The most aggressive regulatory action at the time of this writing is perhaps the European Union's new legislation called the General Data Protection Regulation (GDPR). GDPR replaces a Data Protection Directive (DPD) issued by the EU in 1995, and is much stronger and broader in scope. First, as a "regulation" rather than a mere "directive," it is now the law for EU members. Second, GDPR has the power to inflict devastating penalties on companies that break the law—the maximum penalty being the *greater* between 20 million euros and 4 percent of global revenue. This is a serious cost that will force even tech giants to pay attention.

The complexities of the GDPR can be split into two main sections: *nondiscrimination* and *right to explanation*. The nondiscrimination part asserts that using algorithms to profile individuals is intrinsically discriminatory. Thus, the GDPR bans decisions based solely on the use of *sensitive data*, which is defined to include personal data regarding race, politics, religion, gender, health, and more.

There are two potential legal interpretations of the rules,

both of which pose challenges. In what's called the minimal interpretation scenario, the rules pertain only to the direct usage of sensitive data—which could lead to such a narrow set of applications that the legislation is effectively ineffective. In the maximal interpretation scenario, in contrast, the rules would essentially ban not only sensitive data, but also any variables they are correlated with (for example, someone's address may be correlated to their race or health). This could render most broad applications of data and analytics infeasible.

Which of these two interpretations will prevail—and will the EU be able to define a middle ground that avoids both sets of potential problems? That's a matter that only years of court cases and specific rulings by EU administrators will resolve.

The second section of the GDPR, focusing on the right to explanation, is directly related to the issue of transparency. Essentially, it mandates that users be able to demand the data behind the algorithmic decisions made for them, including in recommendation systems, credit and insurance risk systems, advertising programs, and social networks. Through this legislation, GDPR is attempting to break down one major barrier to transparency, which is "intentional concealment" by corporations. But it doesn't address the technical challenges regarding the transparency of modern algorithms.

The interpretation challenges with GDPR raise a broader question regarding a bill of rights. Is it possible to formulate rules of behavior that are sufficiently broad and generally applicable while also being specific and clear enough to serve as guidelines to action? Rules that are too specific might impose a narrow vision of how algorithms should be used and might also be limited in their scope. But rules that are too loose might leave industry uncertain as to what they are allowed to do.

Experience shows that a bill of rights can be—and should be—flexible enough to be applied with varying degrees of rigor to various spheres of activity. Consider, for example, the guarantee of freedom of speech in the U.S. Bill of Rights. It has long been accepted that the strictness with which this guarantee applies varies from one sphere of communication to another. Commercial speech, such as advertising of consumer products, can be and is subjected to rules and regulations regarding accuracy so as to prevent companies from defrauding customers; businesses can even be required to engage in prescribed forms of speech they might otherwise prefer to avoid, such as the printing of nutrition information on food containers and of health warnings on cigarette packages. By contrast, speech dealing with political and social issues has been granted the widest spectrum of free speech protection so as to make it very difficult for government officers to prevent the dissemination of information of which they disapprove.

Principles of algorithmic rights will need to be similarly flexible in order to strike the right balance between protection and freedom in various realms of human behavior, distinguishing "high-stakes" or "safety-critical" fields such as criminal justice and self-driving cars from less-risky areas such as entertainment or social networking.

———

In September 2016, Facebook, Amazon, Google, IBM, and Microsoft came together to create The Partnership on AI. They were later joined by Apple, eBay, Intel, SAP, Sony, and other industry giants. A range of nonprofit organizations with a stake in the human rights issues surrounding algorithms have also become part of the project—for example, the American Civil Liberties Union, Amnesty International, the Electronic Frontier Foundation, and Human Rights Watch. The goal of the partnership is to study and define best practices for AI technologies as well as to advance public knowledge of AI. According to Eric Horvitz, director of Microsoft Research, the partnership has so far been focusing on four initial areas of activity: best practices for implementing safety-critical AI systems in areas such as health care and transportation; detecting and addressing biases in AI systems; best practices for humans and machines to work together; and social, psychological, economic, and policy issues posed by AI. "You can imagine there are a number of directions we could go with this, and there's excitement about what we can do in what we call pre-competitive ways," explains Horvitz. "We're all on the same page as big companies, nonprofits, and academic partners."

Because it is sponsored by many of the world's biggest and most powerful tech companies, the partnership is an important opening wedge for self-regulation. But it raises a question: Can a truly effective algorithmic bill of rights be implemented by technology companies themselves, or is intervention by government regulators necessary and inevitable?

On one hand, it's natural to be skeptical about the ability and motivation of for-profit businesses to regulate themselves. After all, these companies have powerful incentives driving them to maximize their profits, continually expand their areas of influence, and increase the dependency of customers upon them. Regulating their own algorithms will inevitably make demands upon them that will cost them money and other resources, which is bound to arouse resistance from within the ranks of company leaders. It's entirely possible for the partnership to ultimately end up as a mere public relations tool to defend the companies from public criticism and to fend off government regulation.

On the other hand, it's interesting to note that the U.S. Bill of Rights is in fact itself an act of self-regulation. It represents a series of restrictions on the power of government *crafted and implemented by government officials themselves*. It works reasonably well because of certain clever enforcement mechanisms built into the system. These include the division of powers among various branches of government, which enable one branch to limit and restrain the actions of another, and the right of citizens to seek legal redress against violations of their rights through the court system and through the power of the ballot. The relative success of the U.S. Bill of Rights suggests that, with the right built-in safeguards, self-regulation can work.

What's more, a strong case can be made that, in the world of technology, there really is no substitute for self-regulation in some form, for the simple reason that the complexities of technology are generally beyond the scope of knowledge and control of government officials and ordinary citizens. If government-based regulatory bodies are charged with enforcing rules of conduct in regard to AI and algorithms, they will almost certainly be heavily reliant on outside experts with experience in and strong ties to the industry they are regulating. Similar situations arise in such technical fields as securities regulation, food safety, and environmental protection. In all of these fields, regulation depends on cooperative efforts between the industry and government watchdogs. That's likely to be the case in the world of algorithmic decisions as well.

———

It is time now to start drafting a bill of rights for humans impacted by the growing power and sophistication of algorithms. I believe such a bill can be successful only if users of algorithms—you and I—also step up and play our part. So I am also including in my list a set of responsibilities for users of decision-making algorithms.

I believe there should be four main pillars of an algorithmic bill of rights:

- First, those who use algorithms or who are impacted by decisions made by algorithms should have a right to a description of the data used to train them and details as to how that data was collected.

- Second, those who use algorithms or who are impacted by decisions made by algorithms should have a right to an explanation regarding the procedures used by the algorithms, expressed in terms simple enough for the average person to easily access and interpret. These first two pillars are both related to the general principle of transparency.

- Third, those who use algorithms or who are impacted by decisions made by algorithms should have some level of control over the way those algorithms work—that is, there should always be a feedback loop between the user and the algorithm.

- Fourth, those who use algorithms or who are impacted by decisions made by algorithms should have the responsibility to be aware of the unanticipated consequences of automated decision making.

Let's take a closer look at each of these four pillars. We'll start by examining how to consider the rights of users and responsibilities of companies with regard to the first two pillars: transparency of data and of algorithmic procedures. To better understand these two pillars, consider the four distinct phases of modern algorithms, as outlined by researchers Nicholas Diakopoulos and Michael Koliska: *data*, *model*, *inference*, and *interface*.

The first phase, data, is made up of inputs to the algorithm that may be problematic. So one important requirement built into the bill of rights should be for companies to release details regarding the data used in training the algorithm, including its source, how it was sampled, its prior use, known issues about its accuracy, and the definitions of all the variables in the dataset. Additionally, companies should be transparent about how data is modified or "cleaned" prior to analysis. (This is the domain of what is known as *data provenance* in the computer science literature.)

The second phase, the model, refers to the sequence of steps that enables the algorithm to make a decision given one or more inputs. For example, the model for a recommendation algorithm specifies how it generates a recommendation based on a user's past purchases. (A typical example is the "people who bought this also bought" algorithm that was outlined in Chapter Three.) As we have seen, an algorithm's sequence of steps can be completely programmed by a human being, completely self-learned by a machine learning algorithm, or some combination of the two. The bill of rights should require companies to release specific details of the model they've developed. Reasonable safeguards designed to protect their intellectual property will have to be worked out over time. Any solution, however, should clarify the portions of the logic that are programmed by humans versus self-learned and the relevant variables used by the model. Importantly, it should be possible to explain the rationale for a decision even when the underlying model is opaque, such as in a deep learning model. Emerging research on interpretable machine learning will be particularly important to achieve this. Finally, the bill should allow for audit of the source code of the algorithm when things go wrong in "high-stakes" settings such as healthcare and transportation.

The third phase, inference, consists of understanding how well an algorithm works in both typical and outlier cases. The bill of rights should require companies to release details on the types of assumptions and inferences the algorithm is making and the situations in which those assumptions might fail.

The final phase, interface, is the part of the algorithm's output that users interact with most directly. The bill of rights should require companies to integrate information about an algorithm directly into the user interface to the fullest extent possible. At its simplest, this would involve simply informing a user that an algorithm is, in fact, being used. Beyond that, the interface should make it easy for users to interact with the system to access information about the data, model, and inferences as outlined above. Transparency with regard to these four phases constitutes the first two pillars of an algorithmic bill of rights.

The third pillar is the concept of a feedback loop, which grants users a means of communication so that they have some degree of control over how an algorithm makes decisions for them. The nature of the loop will inevitably vary, depending on the kind of algorithm being developed and the types of real-world interactions it manages. It can be as limited and straightforward as giving a Facebook user the power to flag a news post as potentially false; it can be as dramatic and significant as letting a passenger intervene when he is not satisfied with the choices a driverless car appears to be making.

The fourth and final pillar is perhaps the most complicated one—yet perhaps the most important. It concerns the users' responsibility to be aware of the risk of unanticipated consequences, and therefore to be more informed and engaged consumers of automated decision-making systems. Only by assuming this responsibility can users make full use of the rights outlined in the first three pillars.

———

Michael Kearns, a professor of computer science at Penn and a leading machine learning researcher, recently addressed a group of sixty esteemed scientists at the prestigious Santa Fe Institute. His subject was the insidious bias built into many of the algorithms used for socially sensitive activities such as criminal sentencing and loan approval.

It was a version of a talk that Kearns had given before. But he couldn't ignore the irony of discussing the dangers inherent in new technologies in this particular location. The Santa Fe Institute is just forty miles from the town of Los Alamos, site of the Manhattan Project, where more than six thousand scientists and support staff worked together from 1939 to 1945 to produce the world's first atomic bomb. The ultimate impact of the project was enormous: some 200,000 lives lost at Hiroshima and Nagasaki, and the unleashing of a new technological threat that has loomed over humankind for more than seven decades since.

Looking back at those physicists involved in the Manhattan Project and their response to the social and ethical challenges their work presented offers a valuable precedent. In the years that followed the Hiroshima and Nagasaki bombings, many of them publicly assumed responsibility for their work by taking part in an effort to restrict the use of atomic weapons.

The most famous example is that of Albert Einstein. His 1939 letter to Franklin D. Roosevelt about the potential of atomic weapons helped trigger the launch of the Manhattan Project. Einstein had been motivated by the fear that Hitler and the Nazis might develop atom bombs first, but after seeing the results of the effort that he helped to spark, he was filled with regret. "Had I known that the Germans would not succeed in producing an atomic bomb," he said, "I would have never lifted a finger."

Einstein later dedicated time and energy to supporting efforts to control the weapons he had helped to create. In fact, the final public document that he signed, just days before his death in 1955, was the Russell-Einstein Manifesto—an eloquent call to scientists to act for the good of humanity. Supported by other such notable scientists and intellectuals as Max Born, Frédéric Joliot-Curie, Linus Pauling, and Bertrand Russell, the manifesto states:

> There lies before us, if we choose, continual progress in happiness, knowledge, and wisdom. Shall we, instead,

choose death, because we cannot forget our quarrels?
We appeal as human beings to human beings: Remember your humanity, and forget the rest. If you can do so,
the way opens to a new Paradise; if you cannot, there
lies before you the risk of universal death.

The challenge posed today by modern algorithms may not be
as stark as that presented by the power of atomic bombs.* But it's
hard not to see the parallels in terms of the opportunities and
challenges we face regarding them.

As Kearns reflected on this, his message was a call to action
for the members of his audience: "The scientists who designed
these systems have to take on the mantle to fix them." Kearns
was correct. But his call should be extended beyond scientists
and technologists to also include entrepreneurs, business leaders, regulators, and end users. Together, we have to answer one
of the more pressing questions we face today. How will we con-
ceive, design, manage, use, and govern algorithms so they serve
the good of all humankind?

---

*There are many who believe that the challenges with AI are just as stark. Entre-
preneur and innovator Elon Musk has long been a leading doomsayer of AI. At a
meeting of American governors, he called AI the "biggest risk we face as a civiliza-
tion" and urged that government do a better job of regulating it. But the subject is
fraught with controversy. Mark Zuckerberg called Musk's stance "irresponsible,"
suggesting it was fearmongering. This spurred Musk to tweet, "I've talked to Mark
about this. His understanding of the subject is limited."

Conclusion

The Games Algorithms Play

In life, unlike chess, the game continues after checkmate.

Isaac Asimov, *Fantastic Voyage II: Destination Brain*

istorian and technologist David Nye has argued that "the meaning of a tool is inseparable from the stories that surround it." In the context of artificial intelligence (AI), those stories have been dominated by the games that AI systems play.

It started with Kempelen's Mechanical Turk, the chess-playing "machine." Although that automaton was a hoax, it set a precedent—you could even say, initiated an obsession—for computer scientists for a long time to come. According to the computer science professor Nathan Ensmenger of Indiana University, many in the computing community believed with Nobel

Laureate Herbert Simon that once a machine mastered chess—the "intellectual game par excellence," in Simon's words—"one would seem to have penetrated to the core of human intellectual endeavor."

In 1965, Soviet mathematician Alexander Kronrod called chess "the drosophila of artificial intelligence." By that he meant that the game was to artificial intelligence research what the fruit fly had been to genetics research: a test bed for the field's biggest ideas, at once accessible enough to experiment on easily and complex enough to learn from. Fruit flies are easy to maintain in a small lab, have a short reproductive cycle of one to two weeks (enabling researchers to study multiple generations in a matter of months), and have more than 60 percent of the disease-causing genes in humans. As David Bilder, former president of the National Drosophila Board of Directors, points out, fruit fly research has led in one way or another to five Nobel prizes over the past eighty-five years. Chess, computer scientists believed, could have a similar impact on AI. Ensmenger noted a few years ago, "It is a rare discussion of AI, whether historical, philosophical, or technical, that does not eventually come around to chess-playing computers."

Nor were computer scientists the only people convinced that chess was AI's alpha and omega. When on May 11, 1997, IBM's Deep Blue computer beat Garry Kasparov, the media and public response was enthusiastic. This seemed to prove the legitimacy of computers, demonstrating that they could now emulate, and even beat, humans at a task that was both mathematically and technically difficult—but also one that involved as much art as science. Was Kubrick's HAL 9000 just around the corner?

As the initial excitement settled down, critics began questioning what this accomplishment actually meant for machine intelligence. John McCarthy, the organizer of the original AI conference at Dartmouth, wrote in a piece published in *Science* in 1997 that "Computer chess has developed as much as genetics might have if the geneticists had concentrated their efforts starting in 1910 on breeding racing Drosophila. We would have some science, but mainly we would have very fast fruit flies."

It wasn't an entirely novel critique. In 1990, MIT professor Rodney Brooks argued that the field's obsession with games was problematic in that it anchored intelligence to systems of symbols, rather than to the sort of physical reality that supports and propels human intelligence. "Traditional AI has tried to demonstrate sophisticated reasoning in rather impoverished domains," wrote Rodney Brooks in an article titled "Elephants Don't Play Chess." Programmers, he said, should aim for AI that performs tasks—such as understanding language or manipulating objects in the physical world—simpler than winning chess tournaments, but that operates "robustly in noisy complex domains" rather than in "the sea of symbols" that games provide. The programmers, however, did not heed his advice. Games conveniently offered a setting in which AI systems could compete against the top-ranked humans—and against one another—to easily quantify progress.

Jeopardy! would be their next touchstone. In 2011, IBM's

Watson, a natural language–processing (NLP) and question-answer system built on a supercomputer, set out to beat Ken Jennings and Brad Rutter, the two best players in the history of the hit television game show. Research showed that in order to surpass human *Jeopardy!* champions, a computer would have to be far more multifaceted than Deep Blue was in 1997. For example, turn-taking doesn't exist in *Jeopardy!* Instead, a player has to decide, very quickly, how confident it is that it will be right. It also needed to be able to choose categories and clues, and to develop wagering strategies. Watson was able to manage all those tasks. When the game ended, the computer had won $77,147, Jennings $24,000, and Rutter $21,600. Jennings responded to his defeat with good humor. At the bottom of his Final Jeopardy response, broadcast live, he wrote, "I, for one, welcome our new computer overlords."

IBM later commercialized Watson, and today IBM is trying to apply the framework to assist human practitioners in fields as varied as education, medicine, human resource management, supply chain management, and law.

In 2014, Google bought the UK startup DeepMind, a company specializing in AI research and neural networks, and turned its attention to a new game board—Go. As discussed in Chapter Five, in March 2016 its AlphaGo program beat Go's reigning champion, Lee Sedol, four games to one.

So what comes next? Something trendy like Minecraft? Or a sport that requires both brains and physicality? What game would push machines to new levels of human-ness, in order to surpass humans? The history of computing has shown that what we conquer determines where we go next. After narrow artificial intelligence killed off chess, scientists became more ambitious, once again targeting the general AI many had given up on decades earlier. A computer that won *Jeopardy!* wasn't in HAL territory, nor was even one that could prevail at Go. But the next AI "Drosophila" can nonetheless tell us something about the future.

In a 2005 article for the twenty-fifth anniversary issue of *AI Magazine*, the computer scientist Nils Nilsson claimed that "achieving real human-level artificial intelligence would necessarily imply that most of the tasks that humans perform for pay could be automated. Rather than work toward this goal of automation by building special-purpose systems, I argue for the development of general purpose educable systems that can learn and be taught to perform any of the thousands of jobs that humans can perform." In other words, instead of using the Turing test or games such as chess and Go to measure intelligence, we could use an "employment test" as another measure of intelligence. AI systems would be subjected to versions of real-life, human-focused vocational exams, and progress could be traced by how many of these jobs, from receptionist to geographer to marriage counselor, an AI system could perform. "As the number of tests passed by AI programs increases, so correspondingly, I would claim, does AI progress toward 'human-level intelligence,'" wrote Nilsson. What's clear in his vision is that a "successful" AI system would have to do far more than master the art and craft of a single game. The jobs we do require a much greater range of knowledge and skills than does chess, Go, or *Jeopardy!*

A study conducted in 2017 by the management consulting firm McKinsey and Company investigated jobs that could be automated using current technology. It examined 2,000 activities that were essential to the occupations in question, and its analysis suggested that nearly half of those 2,000 activities could be automated by technology that already exists. Machine learning drives much of this ability.

The Oxford University philosopher Nick Bostrom, the director of the Future of Humanity Institute and its Strategic Artificial Intelligence Research Centre, conducted a survey of the most influential voices in the field of AI and asked when they believed computers would reach human-level intelligence, or AGI. A tenth of the participants believed we will reach this level by 2022, 50 percent by 2040, and 90 percent by 2075. In short, we may not be far from the day when Nilsson's vision of general purpose AI is realized.

It isn't surprising that software systems process data more efficiently than humans. Their relatively new aptitude to achieve human-level performance at perceptual tasks is more startling, but still not the stuff of science fiction. I believe that the most uniquely human of our abilities is to make decisions—choosing between objects, between people, between courses of action.

Today's technologies are advancing into this territory, and the stakes are high, whether they involve autonomous cars or disease diagnosis. As we outsource more of such activities to smart algorithms, it becomes ever more critical that we develop some very human tools—a set of rights, responsibilities, and regulations—to manage and even thrive through our technological innovations.

———

Carol. u got much to do in fix

Ted: im seller cable 130 that it

Ted: hopefulyl a fe wmore get same way and we can team whack it

Carol: we sellers of 40

Bob: I can can i i everything else

Alice: balls have zero to me to me to me to me to me to me to me to me to

I began this book with a bot, and I'll end with one, too. Tay welcomed us into our discussion; Alice will see us out.

The dialogues above are a mash-up of two conversations from real life. The first four comments were typed by currency traders in a private chat room as they tried to manipulate pound/dollar benchmark rates. The transcript was obtained by the U.S. Commodity Futures Trading Commission as part of a probe that led to five international banks being fined a total of $3.4 billion in 2014. The jargon and shorthand make these sentences meaningless to people like you and me, but regulators were able to decode them and identify wrongdoing.

The last two comments are from a negotiation between two bots developed by Facebook. The purpose of the research was to explore whether AI agents with differing goals could negotiate with one another, manage any conflicts that might arise, and arrive at a commonly agreed-upon decision. The bots were shown a collection of items and instructed to negotiate a split between them. Each bot wanted more items for itself but risked ending up with nothing if it could not reach an agreement with the other bot. The bots were programmed with an ability to simulate how the conversation would evolve for every response they considered. If they could negotiate better than (or perhaps less poorly than) humans, it would mark a new frontier for AI.

Researchers trained the bots on thousands of prior negotiation games between humans. In addition, the AI agents also used a trial-and-error method to explore different negotiation tactics in practice games—similar to the way AlphaGo was trained to play Go. And the method worked just as well. While people often get emotional and walk away from negotiations, researchers observed that the bots negotiated harder to achieve an agreement. The bots often feigned interest in items of low value only to later compromise by conceding them in return for something else they valued—an advanced negotiation tactic that people often use. This behavior was not programmed by the developers; the bots learned it on their own.

However, the bots sometimes deviated from standard English during their communications. One of the more memorable exchanges between them was the one between Alice and Bob cited above. Even though exchanges like these appeared nonsensical, the conversations went on in earnest with no sign of confusion, and often produced successful outcomes. It appears that the bots had developed a shorthand to improve communication efficiency. In hindsight, that was not surprising, as it's not uncommon for people in specialized professions—whether traders, doctors, lawyers, or Navy Seals—to generate codes and shorthand to communicate more efficiently. Whereas the people reading the transcript may not have understood the conversation, the AI programs certainly did.

To address this, the researchers restricted the behavior of the bots so that they could prevent them from deviating from standard English. They also had the bots negotiate with humans. Interestingly, most people did not detect that they were communicating with a bot. The bots not only fooled the humans, but the performance of the best AI agent actually matched that of humans.

But it wasn't the bots' success that got media coverage. Instead, it was the unusual exchange between Alice and Bob that attracted attention—an account that could take you down a rabbit hole in considering its ramifications. What is language for? Should AI systems have the right to invent their own? Can we possibly police this? But it also poses a question that is at the very core of this book: Where will we set boundaries when technology's limits aren't setting them for us?

In this case, researchers noticed the issue, intervened, and set the boundary for the AI agent's behavior. That represented one test case successfully managed, but others will inevitably follow, and they won't necessarily be in lab settings with minimal real-world impact.

I recently spoke with James Barrat, a documentary filmmaker and author of *Our Final Invention*. He's been investigating AI and its implications for some time now. At some point in the conversation, the subject of games arose, and I asked him which one he thought computer scientists and their AI systems might tackle now that even Go had been conquered. He sat back, considered it, and finally said something I've not been able to forget: "I don't think there are any games left. The next game is reality."

ACKNOWLEDGMENTS

There are many people to thank for this book. First of all, my father, from whom I inherited my interest in reading and who encouraged me to write a book. I dedicate this book to him. My wife, Prasanna, for her encouragement and for shouldering extra responsibilities at home so I could focus on writing. My children, Aarav and Sanika, who had to unfortunately compete with this book for their dad's attention. My mother for her encouragement and interest in my work. My uncle PG Bhat, who has been a constant source of guidance and inspiration throughout my life. My family, including Commander Krishnan, my father-in-law, Savithri, my mother-in-law, and my brother, Avinash.

This book would not have reached fruition without the help of many friends and colleagues. Rebecca Rose Jacobs, in particular,

ACKNOWLEDGMENTS

deserves special mention. First, she helped me with my book proposal. Later, she provided detailed commentary and editorial inputs on the book chapters. Many other friends reviewed early drafts and shared feedback. They include Marcianne Waters, Thomas Triumph, my uncle PG Bhat, and Fletcher Rhoden. Special thanks to Jay Kirk, who allowed me to sit in his writing class and contributed a lot to my development as a writer. Jay's students also gave me excellent feedback for which I am grateful. Dick Polman provided guidance on how to write profiles.

I thank the entire team at Viking for their help and support. Rick Kot, in particular, was such a thoughtful editor. His assistant, Norma Barksdale, helped ensure that we met key deadlines. I thank my copyeditor, Annie Gottlieb, for her careful work. My agent, Jay Mandel, graciously read and annotated several drafts of my proposal. Karl Weber gave invaluable feedback on my proposal, and seeded the idea behind the bill of rights chapter and helped crystallize it. I am also grateful to Rimjhim Dey and Ben Petrone for their help in getting this book to readers' hands.

I thank my current and former students—Alex Miller, Dokyun Lee, Daniel Fleder, Vibhanshu Abhishek, Amandeep Singh, and Jing Peng—for their feedback and valuable inputs. I thank Alex in particular for many ideas on how best to describe the predictability-resilience paradox. I am also indebted to many research assistants, including Vivian Jair, Imran Cronk, Ruhi Dang, Amitai Bendit, Vid Mahansaria and David Kanter, all of whom helped me in reviewing and summarizing relevant research.

I interviewed many people for this book, including Eric Horvitz, Kevin Gibbs, Pedro Domingos, Michael Kearns, Rene Kizilcec, Ranjani Ramamurthy, Nancy Segal, Andrew Norden, and James Barrat. I am grateful to all of them for taking the time for these interviews.

Over the years, I have collaborated with many individuals: Ramayya Krishnan, Alan Montgomery, Karen Clay, Mike Smith, V. C., John Chuang, Daniel Fleder, Yong Tan, Peng Han, Karthik Kannan, Roch Guerin, Soumya Sen, Ashish Agarwal, Vibhanshu Abhishek, Pete Fader, Andreas Buja, Young Jin Lee, Panos Markopoulos, Anuj Kumar, Harikesh Nair, Raghu Iyengar, Jing Peng, Amandeep Singh, and Xinxin Li. I thank them all for the valuable collaborations. I am especially grateful to Ramayya Krishnan for being such a great adviser, mentor, and friend.

Adam Grant guided me through the publishing process and offered help whenever I needed it. Marshall van Alstyne, Arun Sundararajan, Maurice Schweitzer, Jonah Berger, David Robertson, and Anindya Ghose have been kind enough to walk me through their experiences writing books, and these conversations have helped shape my approach.

Finally, I thank several colleagues at Wharton. Geoff Garrett, Mike Gibbons, and Noah Gans gave me a sabbatical so I could focus on writing this book. Deb Giffen and colleagues at Wharton Executive Education, Stephen Kobrin and Shannon Berning from Wharton Digital Press, and Peter Winicov and his team have all generously offered their help and support.

If I have inadvertently failed to include other friends and colleagues who have been helpful in bringing this book to fruition, I apologize for my forgetfulness. I remain grateful to all those who have generously shared their time in helping me get to the finish line.

NOTES

INTRODUCTION

3 **Such is the warmth and affection:** James Risley, "Reporter John Markoff and Microsoft Research head Peter Lee talk self-driving cars, robots taking the SAT and the AI of Hollywood," *GeekWire*, October 1, 2015, www.geekwire.com/2015/reporter-john-markoff -and-microsoft-research-head-peter-lee-talk-self-driving-cars -robots-taking-the-sat-and-the-ai-of-hollywood.

7 **In 2016, the journalism nonprofit:** Jeff Larson et al., "How We Analyzed the COMPAS Recidivism Algorithm," *ProPublica*, May 23, 2016, www.propublica.org/article/how-we-analyzed-the -compas-recidivism-algorithm.

8 **algorithms that promoted fake news stories:** Abby Ohlheiser, "Three days after removing human editors, Facebook is already trending fake news," *Washington Post*, August 29, 2016, www.washingtonpost .com/news/the-intersect/wp/2016/08/29/a-fake-headline-about

-megyn-kelly-was-trending-on-facebook/?noredirect=on&utm
_term=.9185140ef0f1.

8 **gender bias in job ads:** Tom Simonite, "Probing the Dark Side of
Google's Ad-Targeting System," *MIT Technology Review*, July 6,
2015, www.technologyreview.com/s/539021/probing-the-dark-side
-of-googles-ad-targeting-system.

8 **anti-Semitism in autocomplete algorithms:** Carole Cadwalladr,
"Google, democracy and the truth about internet search," *The
Guardian*, December 4, 2016, www.theguardian.com/technology
/2016/dec/04/google-democracy-truth-internet-search-facebook.

9 **She calls them "weapons of math destruction":** Cathy O'Neil,
*Weapons of Math Destruction: How Big Data Increases Inequality and
Threatens Democracy* (New York: Crown, 2016).

11 **According to a report published by:** Eric M. Aldrich, Joseph A.
Grundfest, and Gregory Laughlin, "The Flash Crash: A New
Deconstruction," Social Science Research Network, January 26,
2016, https://papers.ssrn.com/sol3/papers.cfm?abstract_id=2721922.

12 **According to some estimates, nearly $1 trillion:** Ben Rooney,
"Trading program sparked May 'flash crash,'" CNN Money,
October 1, 2010, http://money.cnn.com/2010/10/01/markets/SEC
_CFTC_flash_crash/index.htm.

CHAPTER ONE: FREE WILL IN AN ALGORITHMIC WORLD

27 **And yet consider these facts:** Carlos A. Gomez-Uribe and Neil Hunt,
"The Netflix Recommender System: Algorithms, Business Value, and
Innovation," *ACM Transactions on Management Information Systems* 5,
no. 4 (January 2016): 13, https://dl.acm.org/citation.cfm?id=2843948.

27 **nearly 35 percent of sales at Amazon:** Paul Lamere and Stephen
Green, "Project Aura: Recommendation for the Rest of Us,"
JavaOne Conference presentation, 2008, www.oracle.com
/technetwork/systems/ts-5841-159144.pdf.

28 **The reason this behavior is so common:** Tristan Harris, "How
better tech could protect us from distraction," TEDxBrussels,

December 2014, www.ted.com/talks/tristan_harris_how_better
_tech_could_protect_us_from_distraction.

30 **Every time a user opens Facebook's app:** Lars Backstrom, "News
Feed FYI: A Window Into News Feed," Facebook Business, August
6, 2013, www.facebook.com/business/news/News-Feed-FYI-A
-Window-Into-News-Feed.

33 **Gelles reported that more than half:** David Gelles, "Inside Match
.com," *Slate*, July 30, 2011, www.slate.com/articles/life/ft/2011/07
/inside_matchcom.html.

34 **In 2012 Facebook conducted a study:** Micah L. Sifry, "Facebook
Wants You to Vote on Tuesday. Here's How it Messed With Your
Feed in 2012," *Mother Jones*, October 31, 2014, www.motherjones
.com/politics/2014/10/can-voting-facebook-button-improve-voter
-turnout.

CHAPTER TWO: THE LAW OF UNANTICIPATED CONSEQUENCES

41 **I'm sure it would have happened:** Liz Gannes, "Nearly a Decade
Later, the Autocomplete Origin Story: Kevin Gibbs and Google
Suggest," *All Things D*, August 23, 2013, http://allthingsd.com
/20130823/nearly-a-decade-later-the-autocomplete-origin-story
-kevin-gibbs-and-google-suggest.

42 **Each of these guesses would be bound:** Carole Cadwalladr, "Google,
democracy and the truth about internet search," *The Guardian*,
December 4, 2016, www.theguardian.com/technology/2016/dec/04
/google-democracy-truth-internet-search-facebook.

52 **A former employee revealed that news:** Michael Nunez, "Former
Facebook Workers: We Routinely Suppressed Conservative News,"
Gizmodo, May 9, 2016, https://gizmodo.com/former-facebook
-workers-we-routinely-suppressed-conser-1775461006.

52 **According to one estimate, the top twenty:** Timothy B. Lee, "The
top 20 fake news stories outperformed real news at the end of the
2016 campaign," *Vox*, November 16, 2016, www.vox.com/new-money
/2016/11/16/13659840/facebook-fake-news-chart.

CHAPTER THREE: OMELET RECIPES FOR COMPUTERS: HOW ALGORITHMS ARE PROGRAMMED

73 **Researchers at Tel Aviv University:** Eyal Carmi et al., "Is Oprah Contagious? The Depth of Diffusion of Demand Shocks in a Product Network," *MIS Quarterly* 41, no. 1 (2017): 207–21, https://misq.org/catalog/product/view/id/1795.

75 **In the first study I did with Fleder:** Daniel M. Fleder and Kartik Hosanagar, "Blockbuster Culture's Next Rise or Fall: The Impact of Recommender Systems on Sales Diversity," *Management Science* 55, no. 5 (May 2009): 697–712, https://papers.ssrn.com/sol3/papers.cfm?abstract_id=955984.

75 **To further test the theory:** Dokyun Lee and Kartik Hosanagar, "How Do Recommender Systems Affect Sales Diversity? A Cross-Category Investigation via Randomized Field Experiment," *Information Systems Research*, October 7, 2016, https://papers.ssrn.com/sol3/papers.cfm?abstract_id=2603361.

79 **Subsequent research by my group:** Kartik Hosanagar et al., "Will the Global Village Fracture into Tribes: Recommender Systems and Their Effects on Consumers," *Management Science* 60, no. 4 (April 2014): 805–23, https://papers.ssrn.com/sol3/papers.cfm?abstract_id=1321962.

79 **as well as a group at MIT:** Erik Brynjolfsson et al., "Goodbye Pareto Principle, Hello Long Tail: The Effect of Search Costs on Concentration of Product Sales," *Management Science*, January 2011, https://papers.ssrn.com/sol3/papers.cfm?abstract_id=953587.

79 **Recognizing the popularity bias of collaborative:** Sander Dieleman, "Recommending music on Spotify with deep learning," Sander Dieleman [blog], August 5, 2014, http://benanne.github.io/2014/08/05/spotify-cnns.html.

80 **Spotify therefore additionally uses machine learning:** Sophia Ciocca, "How Does Spotify Know You So Well?" Medium, October 10, 2017, https://medium.com/s/story/spotifys-discover-weekly-how-machine-learning-finds-your-new-music-19a41ab76efe.

CHAPTER FOUR: ALGORITHMS BECOME INTELLIGENT:
A BRIEF HISTORY OF AI

83 **On May 28, 1783, Hungarian inventor:** Wolfgang Kempelen to
Benjamin Franklin, May 28, 1783, *Founders Online*, National
Archives, last modified June 13, 2018, https://founders.archives.gov
/documents/Franklin/01-40-02-0041. Original source: *The Papers
of Benjamin Franklin*, vol. 40, *May 16 through September 15, 1783*,
ed. Ellen R. Cohn (New Haven and London: Yale University
Press, 2011), 80–81.

84 **By then, Kempelen's machine had:** Nathan Ensmenger, "Is chess
the drosophila of artificial intelligence? A social history of an
algorithm," *Social Studies of Science* 42, no. 1 (February 2012): 5–30,
https://pdfs.semanticscholar.org/c9c7/3fc7ec81458057e6f96de1cba0
95e84a05c4.pdf.

84 **In 1950, the true scientific:** A. M. Turing, "Computing Machinery
and Intelligence," *Mind*, n.s., 59, no. 236 (October 1950): 433–60,
www.csee.umbc.edu/courses/471/papers/turing.pdf.

85 **Nevertheless, the foundation reluctantly gave:** Ronald R. Kline,
"Cybernetics, Automata Studies and the Dartmouth Conference
on Artificial Intelligence," *IEEE Annals of the History of Computing* 33,
no. 4 (2011): 5–16, www.semanticscholar.org/paper/Cybernetics
%2C-Automata-Studies%2C-and-the-Dartmouth-on-Kline/0dad2e
0f8520d81ad0080a7aff45c96e4866c541.

87 **A few months prior to attending:** Hunter Heyck, "Defining the
Computer: Herbert Simon and the Bureaucratic Mind—Part 2,"
IEEE Annals of the History of Computing 30, no. 2 (April–June
2008): 52–63, www.cbi.umn.edu/about/nsl/v24n1text.pdf.

87 **The software proved the theorems:** Ibid.

87 **In response to this tremendous:** Ibid.

90 **Nathan Ensmenger, a historian of computing:** Ensmenger, "Is chess
the drosophila . . . ?"

96 **Given these relatively primitive data:** Ford Burkhart, "Dr. Jack
Myers, 84, a Pioneer In Computer-Aided Diagnoses," *The New
York Times*, February 22, 1998, www.nytimes.com/1998/02/22/us
/dr-jack-myers-84-a-pioneer-in-computer-aided-diagnoses.html.

97 **exercising their five senses:** Luke Oakden-Rayner, "The End of Human Doctors—Understanding Medicine," Luke Oakden-Rayner, PhD Candidate/Radiologist [blog], April 24, 2017, https://lukeoakdenrayner.wordpress.com/2017/04/24/the-end-of -human-doctors-understanding-medicine.

CHAPTER FIVE: MACHINE LEARNING AND THE PREDICTABILITY-RESILIENCE PARADOX

103 **and even though its knowledge:** Murray Campbell, "20 Years After Deep Blue, a New Era in Human-Machine Collaboration," IBM THINK Blog, May 11, 2017, www.ibm.com/blogs/think/2017/05 /deep-blue.

104 **It was trained on a database:** Cade Metz, "In a Huge Breakthrough, Google's AI Beats a Top Player at the Game of Go," *Wired*, January 27, 2016, www.wired.com/2016/01/in-a-huge-breakthrough-googles -ai-beats-a-top-player-at-the-game-of-go.

104 **AlphaGo, playing black, made an unusual:** "Move 37!! Lee Sedol vs AlphaGo Match 2," YouTube, March 12, 2016, www.youtube.com /watch?v=JNrXgpSEEIE.

110 **To be clear, machine learning systems:** Kevin Eykholt et al., "Robust Physical-World Attacks on Deep Learning Models," arXiv.org, Cornell University Library, July 27, 2017, https://arxiv.org/abs /1707.08945.

115 **"Laws and institutions must go":** Thomas Jefferson to H. Tompkinson (aka Samuel Kercheval), July 12, 1816, www.loc.gov /resource/mtj1.049_0255_0262.

119 **In 2001, researchers at Microsoft compared:** Michelle Banko and Eric Brill, "Scaling to Very Very Large Corpora for Natural Language Disambiguation," Microsoft Research, January 1, 2001, www.microsoft.com/en-us/research/publication/scaling-to-very -very-large-corpora-for-natural-language-disambiguation.

121 **In a matter of weeks, from teaching:** David Silver et al., "Mastering the game of Go without Human Knowledge," *Nature* 550 (October 2017): 354–59, https://www.nature.com/articles/nature24270

.epdf?author_access_token=VJXbVjaSHxFoctQQ4p2k4tRgN0jAj
Wel9jnR3ZoTv0PVW4gB86EEpGqTRDtpIz-2rmo8-KG06gqVob
U5NSCFeHILHcVFUeMsbvwS-lxjqQGg98faovwjxeTUg
ZAUMnRQ.

122 **It is no surprise, then, that:** Dawn Chan, "The AI That Has
Nothing to Learn From Humans," *The Atlantic*, October 20, 2017,
www.theatlantic.com/technology/archive/2017/10/alphago-zero-the
-ai-that-taught-itself-go/543450.

CHAPTER SIX: THE PSYCHOLOGY OF ALGORITHMS

134 **In studies from 2010:** Daniel Fleder et al., "Recommender Systems
and Their Effects on Consumers: The Fragmentation Debate,"
EC '10: Proceedings of the 11th ACM Conference on Electronic
Commerce, Cambridge, MA, June 7–11, 2010 (New York: ACM
Digital Library, 2010), 229–30, https://dl.acm.org/citation.cfm?id
=1807378.

134 **and 2014:** Kartik Hosanagar et al., "Will the Global Village
Fracture into Tribes: Recommender Systems and Their Effects on
Consumers," *Management Science* 60, no. 4 (April 2014): 805–23,
https://papers.ssrn.com/sol3/papers.cfm?abstract_id=1321962.

135 **A 2015 study conducted by researchers:** Eytan Bakshy et al.,
"Exposure to ideologically diverse news and opinion on
Facebook," *Science* 348, no. 6239 (June 2015): 1130–32, http://
science.sciencemag.org/content/348/6239/1130.

138 **The researchers found that the vast:** Seth Flaxman et al., "Filter
Bubbles, Echo Chambers, and Online News Consumption," *Public
Opinion Quarterly* 80, no. S1 (2016): 298–320, https://5harad.com
/papers/bubbles.pdf.

141 **The researchers found that simply:** Kiran Garimella et al.,
"Reducing Controversy by Connecting Opposing Views," *WSDM
'17*: Proceedings of the Tenth ACM International Conference on
Web Search and Data Mining, Cambridge, UK, February 6–10,
2017 (New York: ACM Digital Library, 2017), 81–90, https://dl.acm
.org/authorize.cfm?key=N20012.

CHAPTER SEVEN: IN ALGORITHMS WE TRUST

146 **According to some estimates:** Adrienne Lafrance, "Self-Driving Cars Could Save 300,000 Lives Per Decade in America," *The Atlantic*, September 29, 2015, www.theatlantic.com/technology/archive /2015/09/self-driving-cars-could-save-300000-lives-per-decade-in -america/407956.

147 **Yet in an April 2018 poll:** Edward Graham, "Americans Less Trusting of Self-Driving Safety Following High-Profile Accidents," *Morning Consult*, April 5, 2018, https://morningconsult .com/2018/04/05/americans-less-trusting-self-driving-safety -following-high-profile-accidents.

148 **By the end of 2017, independent:** Alex Eule, "As Robo-Advisors Cross $200 Billion in Assets, Schwab Leads in Performance," *Barron's*, February 3, 2018, www.barrons.com/articles/as-robo-advisors-cross -200-billion-in-assets-schwab-leads-in-performance-1517509393.

150 **In 1996, two psychologists at the University:** William M. Grove and Paul E. Meehl, "Comparative efficiency of informal (subjective, impressionistic) and formal (mechanical, algorithmic) prediction procedures: The Clinical-Statistical Controversy," *Psychology, Public Policy, and Law* 2, no. 2 (January 1996): 293–323, https://experts.umn .edu/en/publications/comparative-efficiency-of-informal-subjective -impressionistic-and.

151 **In a survey of approximately a million:** Mark D. Alicke and Olesya Govorun, "The Better-Than-Average Effect," in *The Self in Social Judgment*, ed. Mark D. Alicke, David A. Dunning, and Joachim Krueger, Studies in Self and Identity (New York: Psychology Press, 2005), 85–106, www.researchgate.net/publication/230726570_The _better-than-average_effect.

151 **A survey of faculty revealed:** K. Patricia Cross, "Not Can, But Will College Teaching Be Improved?" *New Directions for Higher Education* 17 (Spring 1977): 1–15, https://onlinelibrary.wiley.com /doi/abs/10.1002/he.36919771703.

151 **And closer to our theme of driving:** Ola Svenson, "Are we all less risky and more skillful than our fellow drivers?" *Acta Psychologica* 47,

no. 2 (February 1981): 143–48, www.sciencedirect.com/science
/article/pii/0001691881900056.

152 **Jennifer Logg, a researcher at the:** Jennifer M. Logg, Julia A.
Minson, and Don A. Moore, "Algorithm Appreciation: People
Prefer Algorithmic to Human Judgment," Harvard Business
School Working Paper 17-086, April 20, 2018, www.hbs.edu
/faculty/Publication%20Files/17-086_610956b6-7d91-4337-90cc
-5bb5245316a8.pdf.

153 **Another interesting idea suggested by:** Robyn M. Dawes, "The
robust beauty of improper linear models in decision making,"
American Psychologist 34, no. 7 (July 1979): 571–82, http://psycnet
.apa.org/record/1979-30170-001.

157 **The same survey question, administered:** Graham, "Americans Less
Trusting."

158 **In fact, the detection of small:** Siddhartha Mukherjee, "A.I.
Versus M.D.," *The New Yorker*, April 3, 2017, www.newyorker.com
/magazine/2017/04/03/ai-versus-md.

160 **This is not to say that all studies:** Andre Esteva et al., "Dermatologist-
level classification of skin cancer with deep neural networks,"
Nature 542 (February 2017): 115–18, www.nature.com/articles
/nature21056.

161 **That's why Chandrashekhar and many:** Varun Gulshan et al.,
"Development and Validation of a Deep Learning Algorithm for
Detection of Diabetic Retinopathy in Retinal Fundus Photographs,"
JAMA 316, no. 22 (December 2016): 2402–10, https://jamanetwork
.com/journals/jama/article-abstract/2588763.

162 **You cannot shout from New York:** Mukherjee, "A.I. Versus M.D."

CHAPTER EIGHT: WHICH IS TO BE MASTER—ALGORITHM OR USER?

169 **Researchers Berkeley Dietvorst, Joe Simmons:** Berkeley Dietvorst,
Joseph P. Simmons, and Cade Massey, "Overcoming Algorithm
Aversion: People Will Use Imperfect Algorithms if They Can (Even
Slightly) Modify Them," *Management Science* 64, no. 3 (March

2018): 1156–70, https://papers.ssrn.com/sol3/papers.cfm?abstract
_id=2616787.

170 **A group of computer scientists:** F. Maxwell Harper et al., "Putting
Users in Control of Their Recommendations," *RecSys '15*:
Proceedings of the 9th ACM Conference on Recommender
Systems, Vienna, Austria, September 16–20, 2015 (New York:
ACM Digital Library, 2015), 3–10, https://dl.acm.org/citation.
cfm?id
=2800179.

171 **"We had somebody":** Rion Thompson, "Chris Urmson Explain
Google's Self-Driving Car Project," SXSW, March 3, 2016, www
.sxsw.com/interactive/2016/chris-urmson-explain-googles-self
-driving-car-project.

175 **The answer is unclear, because:** William Langewiesche, "The
Human Factor," *Vanity Fair*, October 2014, www.vanityfair.com
/news/business/2014/10/air-france-flight-447-crash.

175 **According to elevator historian Lee Gray:** Steve Henn, "The Big
Red Button," *Planet Money*, Episode 642, NPR, July 29, 2015, www
.npr.org/templates/transcript/transcript.php?storyId=427467598.

178 **In 2013 researchers from Brazil:** Natalia Araujo Pacheco et al., "A
Perceived-Control Based Model to Understanding the Effects of
Co-production on Satisfaction," *BAR—Brazilian Administration
Review* 10, no. 2 (April–June 2013), www.scielo.br/scielo.php?pid
=S1807-76922013000200007&script=sci_arttext.

CHAPTER NINE: INSIDE THE BLACK BOX

186 **Researchers have observed that when:** Weiquan Wang and Izak
Benbasat, "Recommendation Agents for Electronic Commerce:
Effects of Explanation Facilities on Trusting Beliefs," *Journal of
Management Information Systems* 23, no. 4 (Spring 2007): 217–46,
https://www.researchgate.net/profile/Weiquan_Wang/publication
/220591412_Recommendation_Agents_for_Electronic_Commerce
_Effects_of_Explanation_Facilities_on_Trusting_Beliefs/links
/0f31753698f5cb6beb000000/Recommendation-Agents-for

-Electronic-Commerce-Effects-of-Explanation-Facilities-on
-Trusting-Beliefs.pdf.

188 **Kizilcec set out to create an online:** René F. Kizilcec, "How Much
Information?: Effects of Transparency on Trust in an Algorithmic
Interface," in *CHI '16*: Proceedings of the 2016 CHI Conference on
Human Factors in Computing Systems, San Jose, CA, May 7–12,
2016 (New York: ACM Digital Library, 2016), 2390–95, https://doi
.org/10.1145/2858036.2858402.

194 **But according to a study:** Wang and Benbasat, "Recommendation
Agents for Electronic Commerce."

199 **According to reports, the primary:** Julia Powles, "New York City's
Bold, Flawed Attempt to Make Algorithms Accountable," *The New
Yorker*, December 20, 2017, www.newyorker.com/tech/elements/new
-york-citys-bold-flawed-attempt-to-make-algorithms-accountable.

202 **researchers at Carnegie Mellon University:** Anupam Datta, Shayak
Sen, and Yair Zick, "Algorithmic Transparency via Quantitative
Input Influence: Theory and Experiments with Learning
Systems," in 2016 IEEE Symposium on Security and Privacy, San
Jose, CA, May 22–26, 2016 (IEEE *Explore* Digital Library, 2016),
598–617, https://ieeexplore.ieee.org/document/7546525/#full-text
-section.

202 **Another approach comes from the researchers:** Dave Gershgorn,
"We Don't Understand How AI Make Most Decisions, So Now
Algorithms are Explaining Themselves," *Quartz*, December 20,
2016, https://qz.com/865357/we-dont-understand-how-ai-make
-most-decisions-so-now-algorithms-are-explaining-themselves.

203 **One such arises from:** Stuart J. Russell and Peter Norvig, *Artificial
Intelligence: A Modern Approach*, 3rd ed. (Harlow, Essex, UK:
Pearson Education, 2009).

204 **In 2016, the Defense Advanced Research:** David Gunning,
"Explainable Artificial Intelligence (XAI)," DARPA, www.darpa.mil
/program/explainable-artificial-intelligence.

CHAPTER TEN: AN ALGORITHMIC BILL OF RIGHTS

209 **In October 2016, the White House Office:** Executive Office of the President, National Science and Technology Council, Committee on Technology, "Preparing for the Future of Artificial Intelligence" (Washington, DC: Office of Science and Technology Policy, October 2016), https://obamawhitehouse.archives.gov/sites/default /files/whitehouse_files/microsites/ostp/NSTC/preparing_for_the _future_of_ai.pdf.

210 **consists of educators, researchers, and professionals:** ACM US Public Policy Council, "Statement on Algorithmic Transparency and Accountability," January 12, 2017, www.acm.org/binaries/content /assets/public-policy/2017_usacm_statement_algorithms.pdf.

211 **The AI Now Institute at New York University:** Alex Campolo et al., "AI Now 2107 Report," AI Now Institute, 2017, https:// ainowinstitute.org/AI_Now_2017_Report.pdf.

212 **One proponent is Ben Shneiderman:** Thomas Macaulay, "Pioneering computer scientist calls for National Algorithm Safety Board," *TechWorld*, May 31, 2017, www.techworld.com/data/pioneering -computer-scientist-calls-for-national-algorithms-safety-board -3659664.

212 **In December 2017, New York City:** Julia Powles, "New York City's Bold, Flawed Attempt to Make Algorithms Accountable," *The New Yorker*, December 20, 2017, www.newyorker.com/tech/elements /new-york-citys-bold-flawed-attempt-to-make-algorithms -accountable.

219 **To better understand these two pillars:** Nicholas Diakopoulos and Michael Koliska, "Algorithmic Transparency in the News Media," *Digital Journalism* 5, no. 7 (July 2016): 809–28, www .nickdiakopoulos.com/wp-content/uploads/2016/07/Algorithmic -Transparency-in-the-News-Media-Final.pdf.

223 **There lies before us:** "The Russell-Einstein Manifesto," Pugwash Conferences on Science and World Affairs, July 9, 1955, https:// pugwash.org/1955/07/09/statement-manifesto.

CONCLUSION: THE GAMES ALGORITHMS PLAY

226 **Ensmenger noted a few years ago:** Nathan Ensmenger, "Is chess the drosophila of artificial intelligence? A social history of an algorithm," *Social Studies of Science* 42, no. 1 (February 2012): 5–30, https://pdfs.semanticscholar.org/c9e7/3fc7ec81458057e6f96de1cba0 95e84a05c4.pdf.

228 **When the game ended, the computer:** Raman Chandrasekar, "Elementary? Question answering, IBM's Watson, and the Jeopardy! challenge," *Resonance* 19, no. 3 (March 2014): 222–41, https://link.springer.com/article/10.1007/s12045-014-0029-7.

229 **Nils Nilsson claimed that:** Nils J. Nilsson, "Human-Level Artificial Intelligence? Be Serious!" *AI Magazine* 26, no. 4 (Winter 2005): 68–75, www.aaai.org/ojs/index.php/aimagazine/article/view/1850.

230 **its analysis suggested that nearly half:** James Manyika et al., "Jobs lost, jobs gained: What the future of work will mean for jobs, skills, and wages," McKinsey Global Institute, November 2017, www .mckinsey.com/featured-insights/future-of-organizations-and-work /jobs-lost-jobs-gained-what-the-future-of-work-will-mean-for-jobs -skills-and-wages.

230 **A tenth of the participants believed:** Nick Bostrom, *Superintelligence: Paths, Dangers, Strategies* (Oxford, UK: Oxford University Press, 2014).

232 **The purpose of the research was to explore:** Mike Lewis et al., "Deal or No Deal? End-to-End Learning for Negotiation Dialogues," arXiv.org eprint, arXiv:1706.05125, June 16, 2017, https://arxiv.org/pdf/1706.05125.pdf.

233 **Instead, it was the unusual:** Paul Lilly, "Facebook kills AI that invented its own language because English was slow," *PC Gamer*, July 27, 2017, www.pcgamer.com/facebook-kills-ai-that-invented -its-own-language-because-english-was-slow.

INDEX